Contents

KU-767-650

Preface

It's been a pleasure to work with Hilary to produce this guide for vocational trainers who work in the further education and skills sector. Hilary's expertise in workplace training and assessment and mine in teacher training and assessment have enabled us to work together to produce something we felt was needed. We share common values of wanting to help people be the best they can be in their role, by giving them access to good-quality resources and information. We both have thousands of followers on social media, and the guide includes many of their suggestions to us.

We are all facing huge changes in our sector, so we think it's important to keep up to date, as well as performing our roles to the best of our abilities. The workplace trainer role is different from that of a classroom teacher and is one that is sometimes overlooked, so this book aims to redress that imbalance. There is often a lack of resources and support for workplace trainers, and this guide will help to fill that gap. We want to enable workplace trainers to recognise where their role might differ from that of the classroom teacher, and how to adapt and be flexible to meet the needs of their workplace learners.

Hilary funds the development and production of all the guides herself using high production values. She runs an independent publishing company and is not influenced by commercial demands from publishers or those with vested interests. Her guides include the real experiences of people working in the further education and skills sector. In the course of our training of vocational trainers and writing resources for the sector, we hear about practitioners' concerns, which we have addressed in this guide.

We appreciate that constant changes can be overwhelming. This guide will help you improve your knowledge and skills as a vocational trainer to help your learners succeed. We hope that the guide will equip you with the confidence and professionalism you need to enable both you and the learners in your care to be the best they can be.

Ann Gravells

70083683

Hilary Read
with Ann Gravells

The best vocational trainer's guide

Essential knowledge and skills for those
responsible for workplace learning

READ ON
PUBLICATIONS LTD

CARDIFF AND VALE COLLEGE

Copyright © Hilary Read 2015

The right of Hilary Read to be identified as the Author of the Work has been asserted by her in accordance with the Copyright, Designs and Patents Act 1988.

All rights reserved. No part of this publication may be reproduced, stored in a retrieval system or transmitted in any form or by any means, electronic, mechanical, photocopying, recording or otherwise without prior written permission of Read On Publications Ltd. This text may not be lent, resold, hired out or otherwise disposed of by way of trade in any other form, binding or cover other than that in which it is published without prior consent of the copyright holder.

Published in 2015 by
Read On Publications Ltd
Home Park
Monkleigh
Bideford
North Devon
EX39 5JY

www.readonpublications.co.uk

ISBN 978-1-872678-29-0

Acknowledgements

Thanks go to Teresa Barker, Professor Ian Favell, Sally Garbett, Mick Gray, Wendy Horrex, Elaine Jackson, Sara Morton, Dilys Taylor, Judith Ward and Phil Waterson for their contributions to this guide.

Thanks also go to employers, staff and learners at KTS Training Ltd for photographs.

Hilary and Ann would like to thank their Linkedin, Facebook and Twitter followers for their help and suggestions.

Photography by James Barke, Bristol

Graphic Design by Eatcake Design, Bristol

Edited by Sarah Chapman, Bristol

Printed by Toptown Printers Limited, Barnstaple

Introduction

This guide to good practice in vocational training is for anyone who is responsible for work-based learners in the further education and skills sector. Whether you are working for an employer, are new to teaching, or working with vocational qualifications, in-company or professional standards, national occupational standards (NOS), or other relevant criteria with your learners, the purpose of training is the same: to enable your learners to reach their full potential and perform their role to the best of their ability.

The best and most effective trainers do this by harnessing their learners' motivation using approaches and techniques to suit the topic they are delivering, as part of an overall plan for achieving learning objectives. This guide will lead you through all aspects of vocational teaching, from planning learning to successful delivery of vocational skills and knowledge. In it, you will find examples from other trainers and learners to help you recognise good practice and to develop in your role as a vocational trainer.

Who this guide is for

This guide is aimed at all those responsible for learning in the workplace. You might be:

- a workplace trainer, mentor or supervisor working for an employer
- new to vocational training
- working with apprentices
- responsible for developing vocational teaching staff
- responsible for the quality of teaching, learning and assessment in your organisation
- a work-based assessor with teaching responsibilities
- working towards a teaching qualification.

Your job role as a workplace trainer will depend upon the type of contract you have. For example, you might be employed full time or part time in the same place of work as your learners. You might be self-employed or freelance, with a caseload of learners. This might involve travelling to different organisations and planning your travel and timings carefully. Alternatively, you might teach in a training organisation or a college, and learners will come to you. You may or may not visit them in their places of work to carry out additional training and assessment.

Whatever type of role you have, you must be in regular communication with your learners' supervisors and other relevant people involved with their progress. Your role will involve using a variety of approaches with your learners that enable them to acquire the skills and knowledge they need to do their job.

In addition, there are many other aspects of your role concerning both before and after the time you are with your learners. This includes planning logically what you will cover during your teaching sessions, preparing your materials and resources, assessing that learning has taken place, giving feedback, keeping records and evaluating yourself and the experiences your learners have had.

Being a good trainer includes being enthusiastic and passionate about your vocational subject, as well as being approachable and acting professionally. Establishing routines and leading by example will enable you to model the skills that learners need to find and remain in employment; for example always starting on time, setting and keeping to time limits for activities and breaks, and finishing on time.

The teaching qualifications

At the end of each chapter you will find links to the mandatory and optional units in the Award in Education and Training (AET), and to the mandatory units in the Certificate in Education and Training (CET). At the time of writing these qualifications were not compulsory, but they are widely recognised by people working in the sector.

Key terms

Learning objectives: Statements that determine what learners do, usually written in achievable and measurable terms using words such as 'explain' or 'demonstrate'

Further Education and Skills Sector: Education and training that takes place outside primary, secondary and higher (university) education and that includes vocational learning through or with:

- commercial organisations (employers)
- colleges
- private training providers
- adult and community groups
- voluntary and not-for-profit groups
- offender groups
- professional and union bodies
- the armed, emergency and uniformed services

Aim: A broad statement outlining what the trainer hopes to achieve with learners

Coaching: A way of guiding a learner through a process or activity

Session plan: A detailed plan that breaks down learning objectives into a structured sequence of activities including timings and resources needed. Sometimes called a teaching and learning plan

---

Key point

You may call yourself a trainer, a supervisor, an assessor, a teacher, a tutor, a lecturer, a mentor or a coach. The term 'trainer' is used throughout the guide to cover all of these roles.

Similarly, you may call those you are responsible for learners, candidates, students, trainees, delegates, colleagues or participants. The term 'learner' is used here to mean all of these. 'Teaching' and 'training' are used interchangeably.

Getting the most from the guide

You will find the following activity useful to identify the parts of the guide that will help you the most.

Activity: Developing your role as a vocational trainer

Assessing where you are now will help you pinpoint the areas you may need to concentrate on when developing in your role as a vocational trainer and the parts of the guide that will help you gain skills and confidence. Where you say you need help with a particular area, turn to the relevant section of the guide.

Question	Yes, I'm confident about this	No, I need help with this	Turn to page...
Do you know the features of training in the workplace and how these affect the way in which vocational training and learning are planned and delivered?	☐	☐	10
Are you aware of legislation and policies and procedures that will have an impact on your role?	☐	☐	20
Do you use inclusive teaching and learning approaches and differentiate between learners?	☐	☐	69, 72
Can you write aims and learning objectives?	☐	☐	32
Do you develop training programmes and coaching and/or session plans?	☐	☐	44
Do you know how to choose and use appropriate teaching and learning resources?	☐	☐	97
Do you know how to embed English, mathematics and information and communication technology (ICT) into your teaching?	☐	☐	51
Do you know your individual learners and what motivates them to learn?	☐	☐	64
Do you know about the following methods of delivery and when to use them?			
Coaching	☐	☐	78
Demonstration	☐	☐	82
Instruction	☐	☐	83
Presentation	☐	☐	84
Group work	☐	☐	85
Projects and assignments	☐	☐	88
Games, icebreakers, role plays and simulations	☐	☐	91
Do you know about the different types and methods of assessment and how they apply to vocational teaching and training?	☐	☐	107
Do you use reflection to inform your practice?	☐	☐	121
Do you encourage learners to do the same?	☐	☐	123

If you need more help in several areas, you can either start with the topic that is most important to you or work through the relevant sections sequentially.

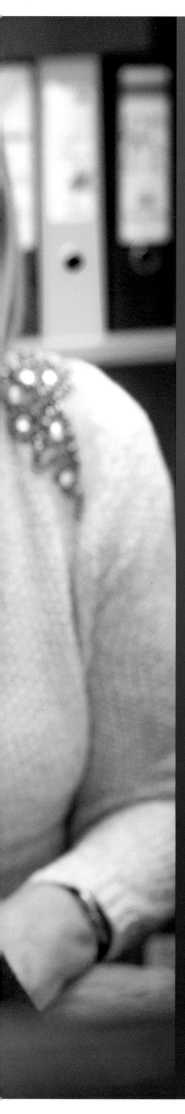

1 Teaching, training and learning
in the workplace

Workplace teaching and learning are not the same as classroom teaching and learning – although the theories of how people learn that underpin them are often the same.

This chapter looks at the specific features of workplace learning and the approaches you can use with learners who learn primarily from doing a job in the workplace. You will find out how to use what your learners do in their jobs as a resource for their training and learning and all the steps you need to take when planning and delivering training.

This chapter explains:

- what the research tells us about what makes effective workplace learning

- the features of workplace learning and how to turn these into practical approaches

- the employer's perspective

- the vocational trainer's role

- the principles of good vocational teaching

- the essential stages in the teaching and learning cycle: identifying learning needs, planning, delivering, assessing and evaluating.

What is effective workplace learning?

From his research into what makes workplace learning effective, Frank McCloughlin, author of the CAVTL Report (2014),[1] found that the key components were:

- the development of knowledge

- the development of skills/practice

- opportunities for practical problem solving and critical reflection on experience

- a 'community of practice' that supports the development of professional identity.

He found these to be the essential elements of successful vocational teaching and learning.

The challenge of the workplace

'[The challenge for vocational teaching and learning professionals is] to build curriculum and assessments that replicate the uncertain, messy, problem-based, people-intense and time-limited world of work.'

N. Hoffman (2011), 'Schooling in the workplace'[2]

The City and Guilds Centre for Skills Development's (CSD) report *How to teach vocational education* (2012) identifies the skills, knowledge and attitudes needed for workplace learners to succeed in their chosen occupations. According to the authors, learners need to be taught the following:

1 **Routine expertise**

   Mastery of everyday working procedures in the domain or occupation

2 **Resourcefulness**

   The knowledge and aptitude to stop and think effectively when required

3 **Functional literacies**

   Adequate mastery of literacy, numeracy and digital literacy

4 **Craftsmanship**

   An attitude of pride and thoughtfulness towards the job

5 **Businesslike attitudes**

   Understanding the economic and social sides of work

6 **Wider skills for growth**

   An inquisitive and resilient attitude towards constant improvement as an 'independent learner' (see page 29).[3]

---

1 McLoughlin, F. (2014), *CAVTL Commission on Adult Vocational Teaching and Learning: One Year On Review*, www.excellencegateway.org.uk/cavtl (accessed April 2015).

2 Hoffman, N. (2011), 'Schooling in the workplace'. Quoted in: *It's about work: Excellent adult vocational teaching and learning*, www.excellencegateway.org.uk/cavtl (accessed April 2015).

3 Lucas, B., et al. (2012), *How to teach vocational education: A theory of vocational pedagogy*. City & Guilds Centre for Skills Development (CSD).

Learning in the workplace

What's different about the workplace? And what does this mean for you as someone responsible for learners based in their places of work? Traditional approaches to programme planning and delivery often concentrate on the classroom or workshop, whereas you need to take a more flexible approach if you're to take account of the context and the job the learner does, as well as what the employer might want. Here are some of the main reasons why this is:

1 **The learner is working alongside experienced workers and doing a job…**

    From the learner's point of view – and the employer's – they are usually learning skills and tasks associated with doing their job under the guidance of someone more experienced than they are.

2 **… so learning is about the main work activities they do.**

    From a relevance and motivational perspective, this is your starting point for programme or curriculum planning. You get your curriculum from the main tasks the learner is supposed to carry out, then plan from there what they need to know and do.

3 **You, the trainer, are planning for the unplannable.**

    This is because you can't predict what the learner will be doing at work, either when you visit them or if you train them in a group. They might all be doing different tasks at work when you plan your training. This isn't to say you shouldn't plan, but it means taking a more flexible approach: for example, being prepared to change the order in which you teach particular topics and taking account of what each individual learner is currently doing. It also means having a contingency plan in case something you planned to do has to be changed at the last minute.

Teaching and learning contexts

A further consideration is the context in which you train or coach a learner. There are three of these: on the job, off the job and near the job.

On the job

This is the workplace context, when you or the employer give the learner direct instruction about how to do something while they are doing the job itself – in the work environment. This usually happens on a one-to-one basis and, whether you are employed by the same organisation where the learner works or by a training organisation or college, the teaching and learning takes place in the workplace.

Off the job

The off-the-job context is where the learner comes to you or is taught in the workshop or classroom – or both – usually away from their place of work. It includes learning that is potentially dangerous and cannot be taught 'for real' while the learner is doing the job, for example, nuclear power control, railway signalling, air traffic control or similar occupations that mean having to use a simulated environment. Alternatively, this might be where the learner attends your training organisation or college for one day a week.

Near the job

This is between the on-the-job and off-the-job context, where teaching and learning take place close to the normal working environment. This might be when learners stop what they're doing and you take them to one side and teach them about a particular aspect of the job.

Key terms

Curriculum: A planned programme of learning – everything the learner experiences as a result of learning that has been planned by you, their trainer

Unplanned curriculum: The unforeseen experiences that the learner may have, such as learning from unintended mistakes and opportunities. It is as important as the planned curriculum in workplace training because the workplace is a source of real-life learning where experiences cannot always be planned for in advance.

This might be:

- explaining how to put together a report at their desk
- practising a skill or procedure
- teaching them about ratios when they're mixing hair dye in the salon
- going through an assignment or work-based project with them and their employer.

The near-job context is an important one if you're responsible for the training in the learner's place of work because it's about adding to, deepening or enriching learning. Learning and progress need to be visible to both learners and employers. This is particularly important if you are a freelance trainer or employed by a training provider because the employer might not recognise the progress being made by the learner or the importance of what it is you're doing with them.

Coaching on and near the job

Below are three accounts from trainers who are responsible for learners in different workplace settings and who coach on the job. The first is responsible for teaching English and mathematics, the second trains digital apprentices via online sessions and the third teaches learners in residential estate agencies. The fourth account gives the broader perspective of a training provider. All their accounts show some of the limitations trainers have to deal with.

'I've built up a massive bank of resources that I draw on whenever I meet with learners. Not just projects but games and real-life stuff that I take from trade magazines or online. I normally go with what they're doing, then make the links to – say – writing something, or calculations from there.'
English and mathematics tutor

'We have a curriculum that we have to get through. My apprentices have to take an online test at each stage of their training before they can move on to the next, so I'm quite limited in what I can teach when they're at work because I'm only allocated two hours' contact time per week. Personally, I don't think it works.'
IT trainer

'My breakthrough came when I started planning real projects with the employer and the learner. It was my learner who suggested he go out and compare board rates with the competition. The employer was delighted and it gave me an "in" with both maths and English because he did a big ratio exercise and a report for his team that they then acted on.'
Trainer, residential estate agency

'We have two hours with a learner to cover both the teaching required and any assessment of competence. To support this, we developed short, ten-minute teaching sessions so that they could be managed in the visit. We also identify any employer training to see if that fits in with the curriculum to be covered, and by completing a sound initial assessment we can discuss with the learner and manager early on whether any further teaching sessions are required so we can then plan them into the programme of delivery.'
Training provider

> ### Key term
>
> **Quality assurance:** The process of monitoring and sampling aspects of training, learning and assessment in order to maintain and improve overall quality and consistency

For more help with structuring work-based projects based on employers' needs, see page 88.

Practical strategies

'It is not a question of whether learning should be practical or theoretical, rather it is a more precise understanding of when, in predominantly hands-on, experiential approaches, theoretical constructs should be introduced.'
CAVTL, ibid, p.110

Here are some practical ways of turning the above principles into effective vocational teaching and learning linked to the workplace.[4]

Strategy	What you can do
1 **Make learning and progress visible.**	Each learner has the job they do uppermost in their mind, and as their trainer you need to make links to other parts of their programme. Workplace learners learn all the time about the job they do, but they often don't know what it is they can do or know without guidance from you in making their learning and progress visible to them. This also applies to qualifications, to English or mathematics, personal learning and thinking skills (PLTS), or the skills of metacognition (thinking skills, study skills and learning to learn skills).
2 **Plan learning around the main tasks that the learner carries out every day at work.**	The curriculum should be what happens in the workplace itself – not the qualifications being targeted. This means that you should be planning and managing learning around what the learner should do or hopes to do, in the job.
3 **Plan assessment and quality assurance strategies at the same time as you plan the curriculum.**	Do this, otherwise you will struggle at the end of the vocational programme – particularly if you follow a tick-box approach to 'delivery' and find that learners aren't performing to the standards in question or – worse – have left the programme because their learning has not been recognised and supported as they go.
4 **Link practice (what learners do) to theory (what they should know).**	Start with the practical work activity and link this to underpinning knowledge (at lower levels) and/or theories and concepts (at higher levels). This is a further factor in maintaining learners' motivation because most learners have chosen to learn in the workplace to get away from classroom-based learning. Nevertheless, the need to understand the relevance of theory to what they do or hope to do by way of employment remains important.
5 **Actively manage the learning programme.**	This is about being an advocate for learners and ensuring that they get access to both the knowledge and experience they need, including: • engaging actively with employers to make sure you provide the right experiences so that appropriate learning is developed • teaching in the areas that have been identified through formative assessment, particularly if the workplace setting doesn't allow for this • teaching the technical knowledge linked to work tasks as they occur naturally and making skills evident to learners as they acquire them • knowing how to apply employment legislation and appeals processes that underpin the workplace, training and assessment, so that you can take appropriate action if all else fails.

4 Read, H. (2013), 'Making the most of the workplace'. *Based on an article published in InTuition* (issue 14), IfL.

Strategy	What you can do
6 **Adopt an individualised approach and delivery methods that fit the context.**	Trainers often deal with learners individually if they teach in or near the workplace. This means adopting approaches specific to teaching and coaching on or near the job. It also means choosing a delivery method that fits the skills, knowledge and behaviours you are teaching.
7 **Involve the learner and learn from them.**	The CAVTL Report (2014) calls this a 'two-way street' and it basically means being both open to learning from your learner and what they do at work and you introducing new or alternative ways of doing things from your own professional practice (both of which make a necessity of the next point).
8 **Teach reflection on performance.**	Encouraging the skills of reflection with learners and asking them to be self-critical are good ways of encouraging them to take responsibility for their own learning and performance while promoting a culture of continuing professional development (CPD). Reflection is also vital for vocational learners working at higher levels because it will encourage them to make judgements and improvements for themselves, both of which are requirements for those working towards supervisory or technician roles. Similarly, asking learners for feedback on your performance as a trainer, coach or assessor allows you to improve your practice by modelling the skills they suggest. For more on the skills of reflection, see Chapter 5.
9 **Challenge learners to continually improve – and allow time for this to happen.**	Deep knowledge, skills mastery and routine expertise mean continual challenge on your part and setting further learning objectives to encourage learners to improve and hone their skills. This is especially important for learners working at higher levels in the workplace. If you are used to seeing qualifications as end points to learning, your learners will not be encouraged to progress further.
10 **Communicate regularly with everyone involved in learning and/or assessment.**	For work-based learners, this will mean involving some or all of the following people: • the employer – or, if you are an employer, your local further education college or a private training provider • the learner's line manager • the workplace mentor and/or supervisor • colleagues in the same department • the assessor and, possibly, the internal quality assurer • those responsible for delivering other specialist training such as English, mathematics and ICT • parents, family and friends. You will find an example of communication about learning on page 52.
11 **Involve the employer in planning, and link your teaching to their organisational objectives.**	Involving the employer as a partner in the learning process provides a rich source of learning activities, for example work-based projects involving real-life outcomes that affect the employer's profitability. In addition, including any training offered by the employer will help you plan a seamless programme without covering the same topic twice. If you already work for the same employer as your learner, make sure the contact at the training provider communicates with you and that you know when they will visit and what's expected.

The employer's perspective

Current government policies mean that employers are increasingly involved in setting and delivering vocational standards of performance. You might already be working for an employer in a training role and be chosen to coach or mentor the learners your organisation employs. If so, you are a key link between your employer and the external training provider and part of your role will be to ensure that the training provider delivers what is best for your organisation and your learners. Alternatively, you may be working for a training provider such as the work-based department of an FE college or a private training company (or both, if you are freelance). Either way, you will need to take account of the broader considerations of all parties if they are to work together successfully.

Here are some more detailed, practical pointers for employers on working with training providers for the benefit of all those involved:

1 **Consider forming a three-way learning partnership that meets the needs of all parties: learner, employer and training provider.**

This means playing an active role and not becoming a subcontractor on behalf of the training provider to enable them to deliver their apprenticeship. Rather, it involves negotiating a partnership where time, resources and funds are allocated according to the agreement reached. For example, if you get involved in government-funded programmes such as apprenticeships, and you take on some of the work the provider might normally do, such as delivering training or learning, you would expect a proportion of the funding to come your way.

2 **As the employer, you are the customer, so expect good service.**

Be wary of training providers that offer existing 'packages' without consulting you: a good training provider will offer to tailor the services they offer to meet your needs. This will mean negotiating and reaching an agreement with them. You will have choices about some or all of the following:

- who delivers the teaching and learning – if you already have in-house expertise and resources, it should probably be you

- the awarding organisation (AO) you use for any qualifications

- which optional units to choose within the qualifications being offered. Make sure that the provider is in a position to offer you the specialist areas of training and/or units you need. This is where your in-house expertise comes in and you can choose who delivers what

- who assesses, including decisions about whether your staff will act as expert witnesses and/or assessors (depending on their qualifications and expertise). This will have an impact on the assessment and quality assurance processes as well as your and/or your staff's time.

3 **Open a dialogue.**

Decide who is best placed to offer which parts of the teaching, learning support, assessment, resources (such as specialist equipment needed to deliver the training) and administration involved (such as meeting AO requirements for qualifications).

4 **Decide how funds and resources will be allocated.**

If you provide training, resources and/or staff time and expertise, you can expect either a share in the funding available or ask for this to be taken as 'work in kind' instead of the employer's contribution the provider might ask for. You will also need to know what the provider charges for such things as:

- training

- registration

- certification

- assessment

- quality assurance.

Key terms

Continual professional development (CPD): The process of keeping up to date with subject knowledge and experience as well as teaching, training and assessment techniques

Organisational objectives: Objectives (or targets) set by the organisation that employees are expected to contribute towards or meet, often to do with productivity or profitability

Training provider: The organisation responsible for training learners, registering them for a qualification and assessing them

Awarding organisation (AO): A body recognised by Ofqual for the purpose of awarding qualifications to learners

Expert witness: Someone who knows the learner and has expertise in what is being assessed

5 **Agree on the procedures that must be in place so that everyone involved is in regular communication, including learners.**

For any qualifications, ask to see examples of the documentation you and your learners would be expected to complete to meet AO or funding requirements. The training provider will advise you on what's needed, but expect them to customise procedures and paperwork to meet your needs and working practices, as these are often generic and may not work for you without modification.

'I thought we'd agreed processes and documentation with the curriculum team but I found out that the assessor had asked learners to complete several lengthy sign-up documents, some of which were written with 16–19 year-olds in mind (our learners tend to be older). We were put under pressure to fill these in. It turned out the assessor hadn't been briefed. I phoned our contact at the college who immediately realised why the documents would not work. He agreed we should complete the two required to start the funding off and that he would redevelop the others for our specific use.

Overall, the relationship has worked because the college leadership has recognised the need to change the way in which things are done. They redesigned sign-up packs, bypassed their usual procedures and have instigated a very flexible service-level agreement. This has cost them money but they see it as an investment in the future – a loss leader.'
National Projects Manager, End of Life Care

'One of the trickiest meetings we had was with the college's contracts manager. She came with two of their standard working agreements. One of these was designed for delivery of the college's existing services, and the other was for subcontractors. We were neither. When I explained that we wouldn't be signing, it almost proved to be a deal-breaker. Luckily, we had already been working with the college curriculum team and the principal was determined to make the relationship work. We agreed the college would draw up a new agreement to reflect the partnership, and that we wouldn't be adapting our practice to fit the existing contracts.'
National Projects Manager, End of Life Care

Activity: Meeting your needs

Choose one of the following checklists and answer the questions according to your role.

Checklist 1: Questions for employers	Yes – and we can prove it	No – we need to address this
1 Do we have commitment at the highest level to enable this partnership to work:		
• within our own organisation?	☐	☐
• from the training provider?	☐	☐
2 Does the training provider have the resources needed to deliver training to the standard we require?	☐	☐
3 Have we allocated roles and responsibilities to appropriate staff?	☐	☐
4 Have we divided up teaching, learning and assessment responsibilities according to our areas of expertise and the resources available?	☐	☐
5 Do the training provider's staff (including any freelance trainers and assessors they might use) have up-to-date occupational knowledge and skills?	☐	☐
6 If we are planning to get involved in assessment and delivery of qualifications, do we meet the requirements of the relevant AO's assessment and delivery strategy?	☐	☐
7 Do we have the necessary occupational skills to develop the knowledge and skills of learner(s)? For example, I'm not relying on members of staff without any recent updating or development, or lacking the necessary skills myself.	☐	☐
8 Have we set up a means of communicating learner progress and achievement?	☐	☐
9 Have I met the person/people responsible for teaching, supporting and/or assessing my learner(s) and am I confident in this person's abilities?	☐	☐
10 Am I satisfied that the organisational objectives have been addressed?	☐	☐
11 Am I satisfied that learners' needs will be met and supported?	☐	☐
12 Have we seen the documentation used and agreed how this will be customised to meet our needs?	☐	☐
13 Have we agreed the division of funds and is there a written agreement in place?	☐	☐

You will need to take action in areas where you answered no. If you have answered no to several questions, this could indicate that the training provider cannot meet your needs.

Checklist 2: Questions for training providers and colleges	Yes – and we can prove it	No – we need to address this
1 Do we have commitment from our Chief Executive Officer/Principal to make changes to current processes, procedures and/or documentation to enable partnerships with employers to work?	☐	☐
2 Are we clear about the services we are offering employers and that there is a demand for these?	☐	☐
3 Have we costed these services so that we know what to charge?	☐	☐
4 Does our approach to delivering training and assessment emphasise employers' needs (rather than relying on generic standards in vocational qualifications)?	☐	☐
5 Have we identified the employer's needs and taken account of their existing policies, working practices and procedures?	☐	☐
6 If we offer qualifications, have we adapted our offer to each employer to include all the optional units available?	☐	☐
7 Have we taken account of any in-house training and/or expertise the employer already offers?	☐	☐
8 Are there sufficient opportunities for the learner to develop with this employer?	☐	☐
9 Does our staff possess the skills necessary to meet the employer's and the learner's needs, including freelancers and subcontractors?	☐	☐
10 Have we allocated funding according to the employer's needs?	☐	☐
11 Have we customised our existing documentation to meet the employer's needs?	☐	☐
12 Do our individual learning plans (ILPs) reflect the employer's needs?	☐	☐
13 Do we have AO approval to offer the qualifications and/or the optional units the employer requires?	☐	☐
14 Have we added details to our centre records of any employer staff who are to assess and/or teach?	☐	☐
15 Have we reviewed our information, advice and guidance (IAG) process to take account of any existing initial and diagnostic assessment carried out by the employer?	☐	☐
16 Have we briefed all those involved in delivery concerning this employer's needs, including changes to documentation?	☐	☐
17 Have we checked we aren't imposing unnecessary demands on the employer (for example, because we haven't checked the qualifications' assessment strategy or because 'we always do it this way')?	☐	☐

You will need to take action in areas where you answered no. If you have answered no to questions 1–4, you will need to develop an overall strategy for meeting employers' needs and upskilling staff before you go any further.

Trainers as 'dual professionals'

You will find it helpful to think of yourself as a 'dual professional': both an expert in your chosen subject area and as a trainer. The introduction to *The Professional Standards* (2014) for teachers and trainers in the sector describes this role as follows:

'Teachers and trainers are "dual professionals"; they are both subject and/ or vocational specialists and experts in teaching and learning. They are committed to maintaining and developing their expertise in both aspects of their role to ensure the best outcomes for their learners.'[5]

This section looks at your role as a professional trainer within the FE and skills sector and what this means. The FE and skills sector is very diverse and consists of colleges, work-based training providers, charities, voluntary organisations, and adult and community learning providers. Vocational education and training (VET) can take place at any time, anywhere, and VET learners can include those aged 13 and upwards who are still at school.

The FE and skills sector includes:

- schools and colleges offering vocational programmes linked to local organisations offering work experience, such as hairdressing, catering and motor vehicle maintenance. The school or college will usually focus on the theory while the work-experience organisation will focus on the practical skills.

- organisations employing apprentices who attend off-the-job or near-the-job training to gain new skills, knowledge and qualifications. The organisation might also be a work-based training provider managing the programme's funding and training.

- companies wanting to upskill their current staff or confirm that their employees are operating to the required standards to perform their role effectively. The trainers might also be employed by the same company.

- charities and voluntary organisations training new staff. The trainers might be working for the same organisation.

What do trainers do?

As a trainer, your main aim is to enable your learners to make progress towards achieving their objectives in the tasks they are undertaking. Your organisation may give you these objectives or you may negotiate them with each learner, set them yourself, or both. A good trainer has a wide range of teaching skills and abilities and can put them into action effectively, in the on-, off- or near-the-job contexts.

5 *Professional Standards for Teachers and Trainers in Education and Training* – England (Education and Training Foundation, 2014)

Key terms

Individual learning plan (ILP): A formal way of agreeing what will be achieved – with target dates – between a trainer, a learner and their employer. Also called a personal learning plan (PLP)

Centre: An organisation such as a training provider approved by an awarding organisation (AO) to offer qualifications to learners.

Information, advice and guidance (IAG): In-depth and personalised advice and support given to learners.

Vocational education and training (VET): Any education or training that prepares people for a trade or profession.

Pedagogy and andragogy: The trainer's expertise in applying an appropriate teaching and learning strategy when teaching young people or adults. Pedagogy is often used to mean a formal, teacher-centred approach to learning, whereas andragogy is an informal, learner-centred approach.

What makes great teaching?

Research carried out by the Sutton Trust (2014)[6] showed the types of trainer behaviour that have the most positive effect on learners' progress. The first two behaviours in the list below have been shown to have the greatest impact:

A good trainer also considers other factors that may affect his or her role and knows when to refer to other professionals for help when these factors are outside his or her responsibilities or expertise. You can look at these in different ways, for example, by identifying:

- your roles and responsibilities

- organisations relevant to your role and those that play a key role in your continuing professional development (CPD), such as the Education and Training Foundation, and/or the Chartered Institute of Personnel and Development (CIPD). Some AOs require trainers to undertake CPD activities on a regular basis and monitor this annually.

- legislation, such as the:

    - Health and Safety at Work etc. Act (1974)

    - Data Protection Act (1998)

    - Freedom of Information Act (2000)

    - Equality Act (2010)

    - Children's Act (2004): if you teach 14–19 year-olds, learners with special needs or vulnerable adults

---

6 Based on: Coe, R., et al. (2014), *What makes great teaching?* (The Sutton Trust)

- Safeguarding Vulnerable Groups Act (2006): this includes the Disclosure and Barring Service (DBS)
- Copyright Designs and Patents Act (1988)
- The Rehabilitation of Offenders Act (1974): if you work with ex-offenders
- Counter-Terrorism and Security Act (2015): if you work with learners at risk of becoming radicalised.
- codes of practice affecting your role, such as:
  - behaviour at work
  - acceptable use of information and communication technology (ICT)
  - timekeeping
  - lone working
- referral points to help with learners' particular needs, such as:
  - basic skills (literacy, language and numeracy)
  - English, mathematics and ICT
  - sight or hearing impairments, mobility needs
  - dyslexia and dyspraxia
  - personal needs that may be inhibiting learning, such as illness, financial problems or homelessness.

The following diagram shows how one trainer represents the influences on her job.

Remember

While you need to know about the many policies, procedures and legal requirements that underpin your practice, they *aren't your job*. Your main job is to train your learner.

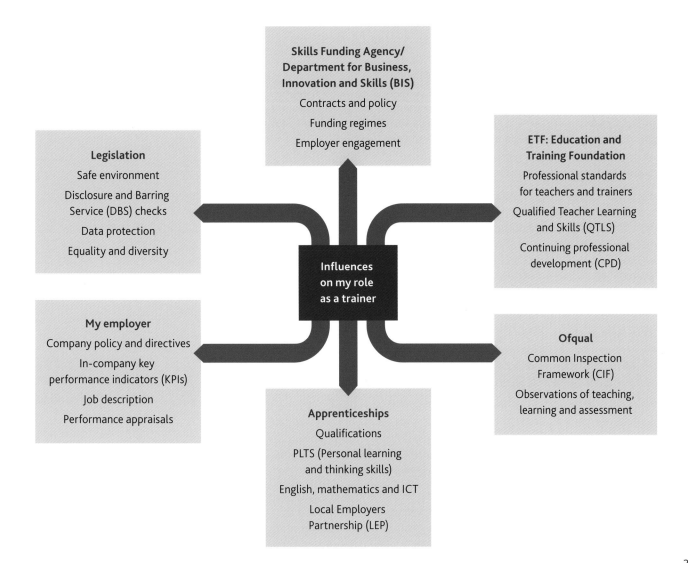

Your role as a trainer

When training in the work environment, careful planning and communication with everyone concerned will be necessary. You might come across some employers or supervisors who are not very supportive of their staff and may put barriers in their way. For example, someone might make it difficult for you to visit your learners at a certain time to carry out a training session, perhaps by changing your learners' shift patterns.

You might feel pressured to train and assess learners quickly because of funding and target requirements, or the employer's favouritism and bias towards some learners over others. Don't oblige, remain true to your role and support *all* learners towards achieving their aims while maintaining the professional standards of integrity and fairness that all trainers and teachers should strive for.

Staying safe

As a workplace trainer, you might need to travel alone to an unfamiliar location in the dark, find buildings on foot, take public transport, or drive to areas you are not familiar with. If you are visiting places on your own, you will be classed as a lone worker and your organisation should have a policy for your protection. If you feel uncomfortable or unsafe at any time, get in touch with your manager or supervisor. Having a mobile phone is helpful in such situations; if not, note where the nearest public phone is should you need it. You may find it useful to search the Internet for the postcode you are visiting. This will give you a street map and pictures of the local area to enable you to visualise where you are going beforehand.

Your responsibilities

Vocational trainers often have different responsibilities from those of the traditional classroom teacher. For example, a classroom teacher might see their learners twice a week for three hours with no contact between sessions. As a workplace trainer, on the other hand, you might see your learners every day if you are in the same working environment. In addition, you may be responsible for ensuring that your learners are performing their job role satisfactorily. You might also have to carry out a training session at short notice.

If you are not based in a classroom or the workplace, you might visit your learners to carry out training and/or assessment at different times on different days. If this is the case, it's best to plan ahead to arrange your visits according to location, for example, visiting learners close to one another to reduce the time and cost spent travelling. Out of courtesy, notify your learner's supervisor in advance, in case for any reason they cannot accommodate you on a particular day. You will need to check travel, transport and/or parking arrangements with them and you might also need to carry identification with you.

If your learner works shifts or during the weekend, you will need to visit when they are working, as it isn't fair to ask them to change their work patterns just to suit you. If for any reason a session is cancelled, your responsibilities will include rescheduling it as soon as possible, and to inform all concerned.

Your responsibility might just be for training and not assessing learners, or it might be for doing both. Whichever it is, it's important to put your learner first and not feel influenced or pressured by external targets, funding constraints or demands from employers. If you have any concerns, you should always discuss these with someone in your organisation before problems occur.

It's helpful to identify what you are responsible for by looking at it from the delivery and assessment points of view. Below are two examples of the different responsibilities you might take on according to your role (there are others). Which one is closest to what you do?

1 The in-company or on-the-job trainer

If you are employed by the same company (which may also be the training provider) as the learner and are responsible for the learner's training and progress at work, your responsibilities might look like this:

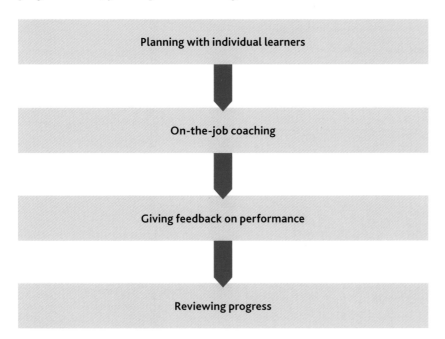

Planning with individual learners

On-the-job coaching

Giving feedback on performance

Reviewing progress

You might also be responsible for:

- liaising with the training provider

- providing expert witness testimony of the learner's performance for summative assessment.

2 The work-based assessor

As an assessor, you are responsible for summative assessment when the learner is performing to the standards in question. These standards could be the ones in qualifications, the organisational objectives, or the key performance indicators in job descriptions. Your assessment responsibilities might look like this:

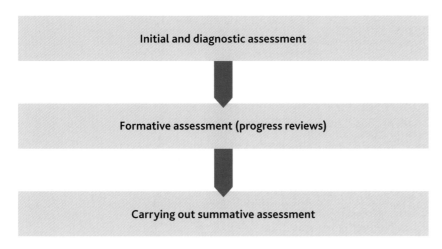

Initial and diagnostic assessment

Formative assessment (progress reviews)

Carrying out summative assessment

You might also be responsible for:

- liaising with other trainers, for example to know when a learner is ready to be assessed, where your assessment judgements have implications for the learning process

- training and coaching learners.

The changing role of the work-based assessor

Changes to apprenticeships mean that assessors will no longer train or coach the learners they assess. Groups of employers in each sector are responsible for defining the career pathways for vocational learners, along with the standards upon which their performance will be assessed and the approaches to assessment. Summative assessment takes place at the end of the apprenticeship.

3 The off-the-job or specialist on-the-job trainer

If you are responsible for planning, delivering and assessing particular aspects of learners' programmes either on or off the job, your responsibilities might look like this:

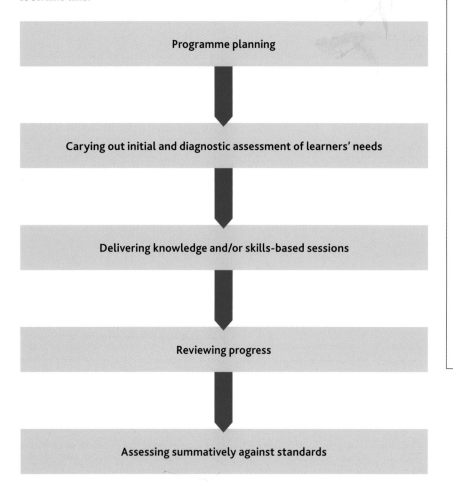

Programme planning

Carying out initial and diagnostic assessment of learners' needs

Delivering knowledge and/or skills-based sessions

Reviewing progress

Assessing summatively against standards

Key terms

Initial assessment: Assessment carried out at the beginning of a programme or session to confirm existing achievements and potential learning needs; often used as the basis for an individual or personal learning plan (ILP or PLP)

Diagnostic assessment: The process of ascertaining learning needs at the beginning or during the programme of learning using an appropriate and reliable method of assessment

Key performance indicator (KPI): A performance measurement to evaluate success

Formative assessment: The process of continually assessing learners to check that learning has taken place

Summative assessment: The process of assessing learners at the end of their programmes of learning using methods such as examinations or tests

You might be:

- a first-aid trainer coming into the workplace to deliver a course

- offering technical training, where learners attend off-job training at their local college of FE on day release.

- a freelance trainer coming into the workplace to deliver English, mathematics and/or ICT.

The teaching and learning cycle

There are five main stages to follow when planning and carrying out your teaching and learning. The stages form a cycle, and you will see from the following diagram that the cycle is iterative: this means that you go round it several times until you have achieved what you set out to achieve with your learner(s). In the evaluation stage you deliberately reflect on the effectiveness of your teaching approach, modify it as necessary, then go round the cycle again with the aim of continually improving your performance as well as your learners' progress and achievement.

1 Identify learning needs

Carry out initial and diagnostic assessment at the beginning of learners' programmes.

Use the results of evaluation and assessment to inform the next round of planning.

5 Evaluate learning

Take account of achievement rates and test results.

Critically reflect on your own performance as a trainer.

Incorporate learner reflections and feedback.

Set personal targets for your own CPD.

Modify your training and assessment practices.

Modify your aims and/or learning objectives.

Modify your resources.

Learner

2 Plan learning

Take account of the employer's needs, key performance indicators (KPIs) or organisational objectives.

Set aims.

Specify learning objectives.

Plan programmes of learning.

Choose delivery methods.

Choose and/or create resources.

Integrate English, mathematics and ICT.

Structure programmes.

Write session plans.

4 Assess learning

Use formative assessment.

Use summative assessment.

Give feedback and support.

3 Deliver learning

Change what you've planned as you go, if it's not working.

Use inclusivity and differentiation.

Maintain records.

Links to the teaching qualifications

Level 3 Award in Education and Training and a unit of the Level 4 Certificate in Education and Training
Unit title: *Understanding roles, responsibilities and relationships in education and training*

Learning outcomes	Assessment criteria
1 Understand the teaching role and responsibilities in education and training	**1.1** Explain the teaching role and responsibilities in education and training
	1.2 Summarise key aspects of legislation, regulatory requirements and codes of practice relating to own role and responsibilities
	1.3 Explain ways to promote equality and value diversity
	1.4 Explain why it is important to identify and meet individual learner needs
2 Understand ways to maintain a safe and supportive learning environment	**2.1** Explain ways to maintain a safe and supportive learning environment
	2.2 Explain why it is important to promote appropriate behaviour and respect for others
3 Understand the relationships between teachers and other professionals in education and training	**3.1** Explain how the teaching role involves working with other professionals
	3.2 Explain the boundaries between the teaching role and other professional roles
	3.3 Describe points of referral to meet the individual needs of learners

2 Planning learning

When planning learning, it's important to have a good overall idea of what you want your learners to achieve. It's essential to take into account the needs of your learners, both in the workplace and in your specialist vocational area. This means planning sessions, creating activities and resources and structuring the learning so that it makes sense from the learner's point of view.

In this chapter you'll look at how you can plan effective vocational training and learning, using some of the theories that underpin learning design to inform the way you structure your learning plans.

This chapter discusses:

- the main areas to consider when planning learning

- ways of structuring programmes of vocational learning, including links to qualifications or other criteria or standards

- the best ways to write aims and learning objectives

- session planning for individual learners and groups

- suggestions for incorporating English, mathematics and ICT.

Planning vocational programmes

When planning vocational teaching and learning, you'll need to know the answers to the following questions. Your answers to these questions will influence your choice of delivery method and the resources you use.

- **Who are you training, and why?**

    What are the individual characteristics of your learner(s)? How will you take account of these in your planning? Are they employed, taking an apprenticeship, attending a day-release programme? These factors will affect your approach to their learning because there may be other things you need to consider and other people you need to communicate with.

- **What do you want your learners to learn and how will you help them achieve it?**

    Is it to do with acquiring skills, knowledge, attitudes or a mixture? Will you use practical activities, demonstrations, discussions, etc? Will the learning relate to a qualification? If so, you will need to have the latest qualification specification from the relevant AO. You will also need to make sure your learner has been registered with the AO. (There is more about delivery approaches later in this chapter.)

- **What stage is each learner at?**

    Are they new to the task, or are they improving on what they already know and can do?

- **Where will the learning take place?**

    Is it on the job, near the job or off the job (on site, in the classroom or in the workshop)?

- **When will the learning take place?**

    You might be looking at two-hour evening sessions, all-day sessions or ad-hoc sessions in the workplace whenever the opportunity presents itself. You might even be training in the learner's lunch break if you visit them at their workplace.

- **How many learners will you teach?**

    Will you be teaching one to one, in groups or both?

- **What are the employer's needs?**

    How will you take account of what the employer may want? Do your learners need to demonstrate their skills and knowledge related to their job descriptions, a set of workplace standards, and/or a qualification? You will need to communicate with the employer and/or each learner's supervisor to confirm that you all want to achieve the same learning objectives. Similarly, if you are an employer, you may want to identify a suitable training provider who can meet the training needs of your employees.

- **What are the constraints?**

    Are time constraints involved, such as needing to fit the programme of learning around work commitments or into a 12-month period? Do you deal with employers who might restrict your access to learners? Do training providers understand your business needs? If you are delivering qualifications, what are the AO requirements you have to meet?

If you are teaching learners skills in the workplace, you can use real-life tasks and equipment as the basis for their learning. Delivering learning in the classroom or workshop, on the other hand, may mean using other techniques such as simulation or role play. A workshop, where learners simulate tasks or work on real projects such as motor vehicle maintenance, is often called a realistic working environment (RWE).

Employability skills

It may be that you plan to deliver employability skills with learners who might be seeking work experience or with those who might not gain permanent employment at the end of their programmes. You will find examples of employability skills on pages 48-9.

Key term

Apprenticeship frameworks: Frameworks designed to meet the skills needs of particular occupational sectors. They consist broadly of literacy and numeracy skills, competence in carrying out a job, technical skills and knowledge, an understanding of the company, the sector, career pathways in the sector, and employers' rights and responsibilities (ERR). Apprentices are aged 16 or over and they combine working with studying for a work-based qualification.

How people learn

Broadly speaking, vocational learners need structured opportunities to:

1 acquire the knowledge, skills and attitudes they need

2 practise them over time

3 gain expertise and become competent, so that what they have learned becomes a natural part of what they know and do in their job role.

Experts in their particular field never stop learning and are constantly looking at new ways of fixing problems or doing things.

The learning journey

The following diagram shows the learner's learning journey. On the left-hand side are the things you do to enable the learner to make progress. On the right-hand side are the stages of assessment. These stages inform your teaching and learning and tell you when the learner is ready to be assessed against standards, whether these are the in-house company standards or the standards within the qualification.

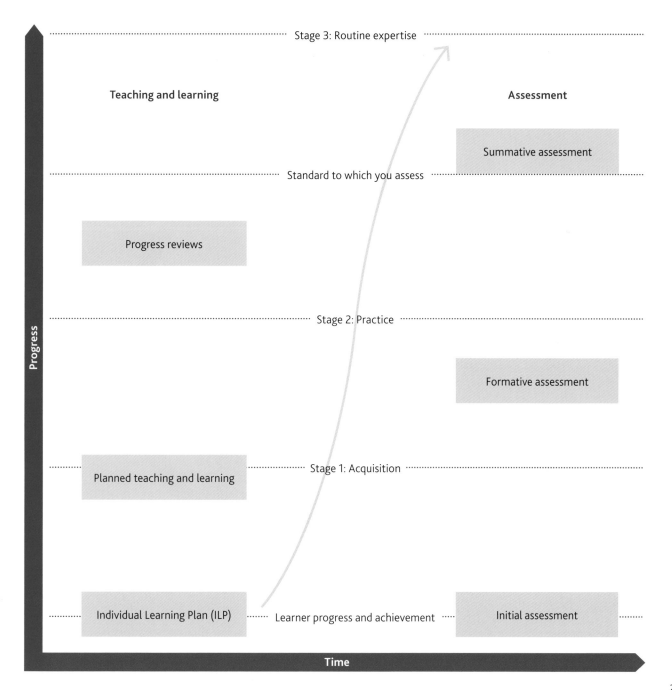

Learners normally learn quickly during stage one, the acquisition stage, when knowledge and skills are new to them. This stage is the steepest part of the learning curve, but the next two stages are just as important. Practice does make perfect: learners need opportunities to put what they have learned into practice if they are to hone their skills and gain new insights (and you need to build in regular progress checks to make sure they are practising the right things). They also need time and opportunities for learning to become part of them – this is the third stage, where learners gain routine expertise over their learning and become competent. Their learning at this stage concerns them becoming an expert in their field and continues throughout their vocational career.

The line drawn across the learning journey at the summative assessment stage is where the vocational learner is regularly performing to the agreed standards – whether these are the company standards or those in the vocational qualification. At this point, the learner's knowledge and performance can be assessed against the standards in question after the acquisition and practice stages.

As the trainer, your job is to plan a programme of learning to help your learner to progress through these stages of the learning journey.

The stages of learning

The following example of 'learning to drive' illustrates the way in which learners move through the different stages of skills' learning, from unconscious incompetence to routine expertise.[7] This helps them to build upon what they already know and can do.

Remember

If you are responsible for both assessing and teaching and learning, it can be tempting to carry out summative assessment too soon – perhaps the first time you see your learner doing something correctly. Beware of this 'tick-box' approach: if you encourage learners to produce evidence of their competence too early, there is a danger that they have not had enough time to fully acquire and practise the relevant skills and knowledge.

1 Unconscious incompetence

This occurs at the beginning of learning: the learner driver knows they need to learn how to drive, but doesn't know what they don't know.

2 Conscious incompetence

Here, the learner driver starts to become aware of all the things they can't do yet, and all the things they need to practise.

3 Conscious competence

Gradually, through practising, the learner driver starts to develop their driving skills but they still need to think carefully about what they're doing, such as thinking 'mirror, signal, manoeuvre' each time they make a move.

4 Unconscious competence (routine expertise)

This is the point at which the learner is totally competent: their driving skills have developed to such an extent that they don't have to think in detail about what they are doing. They set off on a journey, get to their destination and realise they haven't thought about their driving on the way.

---

7   Peter, L. J. and Hull, R. (1969), *The Peter Principle: Why things always go wrong.* New York: William Morrow & Co.

For work-based learners, the final stage is where they become competent at their jobs. It's important not to treat these stages as permanent ones, however, because once the learner has achieved routine expertise they can sometimes slip back a stage. As the trainer, you will need to encourage learners to maintain consciousness of their competence (think of expert drivers with 20 years' experience who still have accidents caused by inattention or basic errors). However, if a learner changes their job role, they may go back to stage one until they master the new skills required.

While the subject matter – what you are teaching – will affect the way you structure learning, each stage of the learning process might also affect the approach and delivery method you choose. For example, teaching new skills probably means demonstrating and instructing, whereas when learners are practising those skills or wanting to improve on them, you will want to use coaching to help them improve, and questioning to check their knowledge. (For more on demonstrating, instructing and coaching, see Chapter 3, 'Delivering learning'.)

The following example from the construction industry shows how both the area of learning and the stage of learning influence programme design:

'We have all our learners in the workshop for six weeks at the beginning of each programme. This is so we can teach them the basics: not just the skills but the routines like the tools of the trade, and health and safety. They get to practise once they go out on site for two days a week. At this stage we have them in for more intensive skills training. They do some classroom-based learning for a half-day a week – English and maths, mainly. We don't start assessing them until we know they are performing proficiently against national standards.'
Construction trainer

Setting aims and learning objectives

If you are responsible for planning learning, you will need to be able to set aims and learning objectives. Aims are starting points for structuring your overall training programme and for identifying and sequencing sessions. They are what you want to accomplish with your learners. You also need to specify your learning objectives – what you want your learners to achieve through your sessions – as the basis for assessing learners' progress (see Chapter 4, 'Assessing learning').

Setting aims

When you start to plan what you will teach, it's helpful to have in mind an idea of where you want your learners to get to. Aims can be broad, cover a lot of skills and knowledge and aren't always easily measurable. For example, learners may aim to:

- drive an HGV

- lay bricks

- provide personal care for the frail and elderly

- operate the company's phone system.

You may not have a say in setting aims: you may be given them by the learner's employer or as part of a qualification, or be working towards in-company aims and asked to plan a series of sessions around them.

How do you set an aim?

One way of setting an aim is to break down the task or topic you have to teach into what the learners need to be able to know, the skills they need and/or the attitude you want them to display.

The following table shows an example written by a group of new trainers when asked what their job involved. You can see how a task or job breakdown gives you the starting point for your aims. By grouping common areas of knowledge, skills and attitude, you can start to identify module or topic areas and set an aim for each one.

The trainer's job

Knowledge	Skills	Attitude
Trainers need to know:	Trainers need to be able to:	Trainers need to:
• their subject	• present knowledge	• show enthusiasm for their subject
• how people learn	• demonstrate skills	• encourage learners
• the theories that underpin teaching and learning	• model the attitudes they are teaching	• be inspirational
• their own biases and preferences and the potential impact of these.	• plan and deliver sessions	• have the ability to teach to the learner's level
	• give feedback	• be able to self-assess and learn from each session to enhance the next one.
	• assess learning.	

Once you've decided on your aims, you can group them into topic areas and put them into a logical order. This gives you the overall shape of your course or programme of learning; you'll need this when you come to session planning.

Another starting point is to look at the units of assessment or learning, if you have access to these. For example, you will find these explained in detail in the AO's qualification specification, which outlines everything that should be delivered and assessed. However, it will be up to you and your learner to decide in what order it's done. Be careful not to base your whole programme of learning on each unit, as the units will be broken down into discrete modules and standards for assessment purposes. You will need to take a holistic approach, taking account of several units at once, grouping topics and identifying the order in which learners need to learn – and revisit the units regularly. You will find an example of how to do this on page 40.

Key term

Holistic planning: Planning teaching and learning across several units within a qualification (or company standards) by grouping them into topics, rather than teaching them one at a time

Setting learning objectives

The next step is to break down your aim into a series of smaller steps and use these to help you shape your sessions and specify learning objectives from the learner's point of view. Here is an example of the process to go through.

Aim	Learners will operate the phone system
Smaller steps	Learners will: 1 answer a call using the company phone system 2 greet callers appropriately 3 know the procedure for placing callers on hold 4 transfer a call.

These tell you the content of your session, but not whether your learners were successful. That's because there isn't enough detail. To write good learning objectives, you need to be specific about:

- the knowledge, skill or attitude you want your learners to demonstrate
- the conditions under which you want them to perform
- the standard to which you want them to perform.

The following two sets of learning objectives are linked to step 2 above, 'greet callers appropriately'. See if you can spot the differences between them:

Set 1 learning objectives	Set 2 learning objectives
Learners will: • give two reasons why using an appropriate tone of voice is important when greeting callers • identify the three elements of an appropriate tone of voice • adopt an appropriate tone when answering calls under role-play conditions.	For learners to: • demonstrate an appropriate tone of voice when dealing with every caller • use the company greeting on all occasions • ask each caller an appropriate question to determine how to route the call.

The difference is in the objectives themselves: the first set is about knowledge of the task whereas the second set concerns actual performance. You'll have noticed, too, that the standard and conditions are different: in the first, learners are more likely to be in the classroom or training room and to achieve the second they would need to perform on the job under simulated or real-life conditions.

These learning objectives are all to do with learners adopting and using the right attitude with callers. Setting learning objectives in terms of promoting a certain attitude is always tricky because you need to be very clear about the values and behaviour you want your learners to display.

Don't let this put you off, though: having the 'right' attitude is often the key to success in the work-based sectors.

'In my area, attitude is the most important of all. If my learners don't adopt the right attitude with customers, they'll never get them to buy anything. This is why recognising and responding to customer behaviour and creating a rapport is such an important part of their training.'
Retail trainer

SMART learning objectives

A useful way of checking that you have written a good learning objective is to use the SMART acronym. SMART objectives are:

Specific: they say exactly what you want the learner to achieve

Measurable: they contain a specific outcome that can be measured so that it's clear when the learner has achieved it

Achievable: challenging for the individual learner, but within their reach

Relevant: to the learner, their job role and the qualification (if applicable)

Time-bound: they indicate how long it should take the learner to achieve them.

Domains and taxonomies of learning

Educationalists such as Robert Gagne (1985) and Benjamin Bloom (1956) theorised that there are different types and levels of learning and that these should influence instructional design. According to them, the three main areas (domains) of learning are:

1 **Cognitive (knowing)**

The cognitive domain is knowledge- or mind-based. As you teach, you will want your learners to progress through knowing and recalling factual information, to understanding and analysing concepts, until they are thinking for themselves and fully understanding what they are doing and why.

2 **Psychomotor (doing)**

The psychomotor domain is based around skills: the learner normally produces a product as a result of the teaching or performs a task in a set way.

3 **Affective (attitudes, values and behaviours)**

The affective domain concerns how and why learners behave in particular ways. It is based on their values or attitudes to certain tasks. Learners should be able to demonstrate that they have the necessary values and attitudes when performing their job role.

Trainers can use domain theory to help identify and prioritise the area(s) of learning that need to be taught. Certain domains predominate in different vocational areas and it can be easy to overlook a particular domain that may be important.

'In End of Life Care the emotional support you offer is as important as the physical care you give. When we teach, we're looking at behaviours in the affective domain such as developing emotional resilience. Through formal supervision, for example, we teach learners to recognise and deal with their own emotional responses by encouraging them to talk through their experiences.'
Trainer, End of Life Care

Key term

Domain of learning: The area that influences or dominates the topic you are teaching. If you are teaching a skill, this is predominantly within the psychomotor domain (i.e. 'doing'). If you are teaching associated knowledge and theory, this is to do with the cognitive domain (i.e. 'knowing'). If you want learners to be able to demonstrate particular behaviours, values or attitudes, this is the affective domain.

Activity: What domain am I teaching in?

Choose a topic or area that you are currently teaching to learners.
Answer the questions below to see which learning domain predominates.

Question	Yes	No
1 Do learners have to learn on the job?	☐	☐
2 Do learners need certain values or beliefs to succeed?	☐	☐
3 Are speed and accuracy important?	☐	☐
4 Does the topic involve knowing certain facts?	☐	☐
5 Do I assess using methods other than tests of their knowledge?	☐	☐
6 Are learners' attitudes vital?	☐	☐
7 Do learners have to understand concepts and apply them?	☐	☐

Questions 1, 3 and 5 are to do with skills teaching (the psychomotor domain).
Questions 2 and 6 are concerned with attitudes (the affective domain). Questions 4
and 7 are about knowledge (the cognitive domain).

Don't worry if you ticked a mixture; most teaching topics involve more than
one domain. This also shows that each domain is important, and although skills
(psychomotor) teaching certainly involves knowing things too, it chiefly entails
'doing' elements such as speed, accuracy and needing to learn on the job, which
mean that this domain is the main one. Teaching and learning in the affective
domain are particularly vital in certain sectors such as care or customer service.

You will find out more about how to structure learning in the section on
session planning on page 44.

Taxonomies

Taxonomies are simply categories (or hierarchies) that help trainers
understand and define the learning that might be expected within each
learning domain. They are useful tools for both trainers and learners.
Benjamin Bloom[8] created a taxonomy concerned with the cognitive
domain, that is, knowledge and understanding. It starts with the 'concrete'
– knowing and remembering facts – and moves on to more complex and
'abstract' skills such as the ability to analyse and synthesise information,
through to evaluation. There are other taxonomies of learning, but Bloom's
is widely recognised.

*'In personal training, you teach the theories behind the different training
methods in the cognitive domain, then move to the psychomotor domain
where learners practise the methods and how you deliver them when
working with clients.'*

Personal trainer

---

8   Bloom, B. S., ed. (1956), *Taxonomies of educational goals: Guide I, Cognitive domain.* New York:
    Longmans Green. Adapted by permission of the publisher.

The following list of the main categories in Bloom's taxonomy gives examples of the different levels of knowledge and understanding you would expect your learner to demonstrate and examples of verbs to use when writing your learning objectives at each stage. Use the categories to set learning objectives at the appropriate level for your learners and to ensure that they progress to higher challenges as they learn.

Bloom's taxonomy

Category	You would expect your learner to ...	Examples of words to use when writing learning objectives
1 Knowledge	• demonstrate knowledge and recall of events, places or dates, major ideas or subject matter	*list, examine, tell, show, label, describe, who, why, what, when*
2 Understanding	• grasp meaning; translate knowledge into a new context • interpret facts; compare and contrast • infer causes and predict consequences	*interpret, discuss, predict, summarise, associate, estimate situations*
3 Application	• use information, methods, theories and concepts in new situations • solve problems using required skills or knowledge	*demonstrate, apply, discover, experiment, show, classify, calculate, illustrate*
4 Analysis	• see patterns and identify components • recognise hidden meanings	*explain, infer, compare, select, classify, arrange*
5 Synthesis	• use old ideas to create new ones; generalise from given facts • relate knowledge from several areas, predicting and drawing conclusions	*what if, create, integrate, modify, rewrite, generalise, substitute, plan, invent, design*
6 Evaluation	• compare and discriminate between ideas • assess value • make choices based on reasoned argument • verify the value of evidence • recognise subjectivity	*assess, decide, recommend, conclude, summarise, convince, judge, support, grade, test, measure*

There are also taxonomies of learning in the other domains. Here are some further examples to help you with setting learning objectives:

Learning domain	Words to use when writing learning objectives
Skills/doing: The verbs you use when setting skill-based objectives will depend on the specialist skills and tasks that learners are expected to perform in their subject area.	*assemble/dismantle, construct, draw, sew, write*
Attitude: The verbs and phrases to use when setting objectives to do with adopting a particular attitude. They are organised according to the principle of internalisation, starting with the learner's awareness and ending at a point where their attitude or behaviour becomes part of their role.	*accept, show awareness of, listen for, respond to, comply with, follow, value, display, exhibit, examine, underpin, require, rate highly, manage, integrate*

Creating a scheme of work

'[Vocational] trainers situate theory in practical examples. They ... put to use the "live" knowledge [brought] from learners into the classroom and workshop.'[9]

The overall plan for teaching and learning is called a scheme of work or programme of work and it is an outline of how all the teaching and learning requirements will be covered within the time frame of the programme. Planning vocational training is different from planning teaching in the traditional classroom, in that you are often dealing with learners from a variety of workplace settings. In addition, you don't always have to fit the scheme of work into the academic year – although you may well be under different time pressures such as fitting an apprenticeship programme into 12 months.

The following examples show various ways of approaching the planning of vocational programmes. Example 1 shows a traditional scheme of work that might be used in an off-the-job environment. If you are new to vocational training, you might wish to start here.

You will find help with writing detailed session plans on page 44.

---

9 McCloughlin, F. (2013), *It's about work ... Excellent adult vocational teaching and learning.* Centre for Adult Vocational Teaching and Learning (CAVTL), LSIS.

1 Planning a traditional scheme of work

The following example is an extract from a simple scheme of work showing the first and ninth sessions and one practical assessment.

Trainer:	A. N. Other	Venue:	Near job: Academy training room A309
Programme:	Wiring and testing electrical circuits	Group composition:	Ten full-time apprentices with no previous knowledge of electrical wiring/testing
Dates:	25 May– 29 June, 8 a.m.–4 p.m.	Number of sessions:	20
Assessment:	Three practical assessments following learning and practice sessions	Aim of programme:	To enable learners to wire and test electrical circuits

Dates	Learners will:	Session content and activities	Teaching/learning method and resources	Assessment
Session 1 25 May	• Gain an overview of the programme	• Overview of the programme • Introduction to session objectives • Explanation of practical assessments	Lecture Smartboard Group discussion	Q&A
	• Describe the causes and effects of electric shock	• Common causes and effects of electric shock	Lecture Smartboard Handouts	Observation Q&A
	• Calculate current and select appropriate cables	• Ohms Law • Calculating current using lighting, motors, showers and cookers • Cable colour codes, types and uses and identification methods	Lecture followed by individual activity Pens, paper and calculators	Q&A Examination of product
	• Explain volts drop • Calculate volts drop	• Explanation of the process followed by calculations	Lecture followed by individual activity Pens, paper and calculators	Q&A Examination of product
	• Explain circuit protection: methods of isolation, locking off and proving dead	• Lecture on how to protect, isolate, lock off and prove dead • Point out these processes/features during visit to the workshop	Lecture followed by visit to the workshop Smartboard, coloured pens	Observation Q&A
	• Identify different tools and their uses	• Practical look at different types of tools and how to use them	Demonstration Tools	Observation Q&A
	• Wire a three-pin plug using the right fuse	• Follow instructions given in the demonstration and on the handout to wire and fuse a three-pin plug correctly	Instruction and demonstration followed by individual activity Handout, tools, plugs, cable, fuses	Observation Q&A Examination of product
	• Describe the use of terminal block, selecting, mounting and terminating cables	• Activity to select, mount and connect cables following a drawing	Demonstration followed by individual activity Tools, terminal block, cable	Observation Q&A Examination of product

Dates	Learners will:	Session content and activities	Teaching/learning method and resources	Assessment
Session 9 4 June	• Describe a power circuit • Recognise the three different types of circuit • Identify the key features and differences between them	• Explanation of two types of radial and ring circuits and their limitations • Component types and identification • Testing and recording	Lecture and demonstration Smartboard Coloured pens Test equipment Test sheets	Observation Q&A
	• Construct an A2 radial circuit in flat twin and earth/ plastic sockets	• Construct an A2 radial using the correct MCB and cable clips	Lecture Smartboard Individual activity Tutor guidance & support Tools components, cables test equipment, test & inspection sheets	Observation Q&A Examination of product
	• Explain how to test a radial power circuit	• Test equipment & methods	Demonstration Smartboard Coloured pens Cable test equipment and test sheets	Observation Q&A
	• Test the completed circuit	• Carry out testing & complete inspection and test sheets	Individual activity with tutor guidance & support Test equipment & test sheets	Observation Q&A Examination of product

Dates	Learners will:	Session content and activities	Teaching/learning method and resources	Assessment
Session 18 27 June	• Construct a control panel from the drawing supplied, using the wall-mounted box	• Construct the circuit using all techniques acquired during the programme • Identify the deliberate mistakes on the drawing and correct them • Carry out testing • Complete the test sheets correctly	Wall-mounted boards Test equipment Test sheets	Observation Q&A Examination of product

2 Planning learning linked to qualifications

If you work with vocational qualifications, the standards, units or modules they contain are those of *assessment*. They are not the programme of teaching and learning, but the criteria that the learner must successfully achieve. Use them to check that you have covered everything, but you should also be using your own expertise in the vocational area and of the job itself to help you plan what needs to be taught and the order in which these topics should be covered. Remember, too, the needs of your particular learner(s). You will also need to plan your assessment strategy at the same time as you plan the curriculum or programme so that you meet AO requirements.

The following example of a scheme of work shows the sessions that make up days 1 and 2 of an eight-day teaching programme linked to the Level 3 Certificate in End of Life Care (EOLC). It shows how the trainers have planned to teach topics linked to the units and assessment criteria within the qualification by colour-coding them. The table following this shows the main assessment tasks and where these can be found in the learner's portfolio.

> ### Key terms
>
> **Assessment strategy:** How you propose to check that your learners have achieved what they are meant to
>
> **Portfolio:** The place where a learner keeps the assessed evidence to meet the requirements of a qualification. A portfolio can contain paper-based evidence, such as written assignments, or be an e-portfolio where the learner uploads their evidence digitally, or it can be a mixture of both.

Level 3 Certificate in Working in End Of Life Care

Key to units and assessment criteria

301: Understand how to provide support when working in EOLC
302: Managing symptoms in EOL
303: Understand ACP
304: Support spiritual wellbeing
305: Support individuals with loss and grief before death
306: Understand how to support individuals during the last days of life
307: EOL and dementia care
310: Support individuals with specific communication needs

Day 1	Topic	Learning objectives/ rationale	Unit/ assessment criteria	Resources
AM	**Welcome and introductions** Icebreaker activity, ground rules	To get to know one another and to set ground rules		Flipchart, group work
	Learning and assessment What is learning? Fears about studying	Give out folders and handouts	310: 3.1, 3.2, 3.4, 4.2	
	Defining end of life care Approach Challenges, barriers How own beliefs and values can impact delivery of EOLC Dignity & compassion	Setting the scene regarding the course To explain the main components of EOLC delivery To articulate own beliefs and values and how these might influence delivery	301: 2.3, 4.1 305: 3.1	Group work, flipcharts, PowerPoint, DVD
Lunch				
PM	**National drivers: general overview** EOLC Strategy, dementia, care of frail elderly	To list approaches to EOLC (1)	301: 1.1, 4.3 302: 1.1 303: 1.3 307: 1.1	Group work, PowerPoint
	Introduction to tools Current approaches GSF, ICP, Amber Care Bundle, ACP	To describe approaches to EOLC (2)	301: 1.2, 1.3 306: 3.3	Group work, PowerPoint

Day 2	Topic	Learning objectives/ rationale	Unit/ assessment criteria	Resources
AM	**What would I want if I were dying?** The main steps: importance, impact, environment, verbal and non-verbal, methods, unmet needs, barriers, use of aids, cues	To list communication factors and establish communication needs Identify ways of addressing these and of promoting communication Be able to promote communication between individuals and others Describe ways of supporting the use of communication technology and aids	310: 1.1 – 1.6 2.1 – 2.3 3.1 – 3.4 4.1 – 4.4 5.1 – 5.2 6.1 – 6.3	PowerPoint, DVD, small group work
	The advanced care plan (ACP) Difference between the ACP and a support plan, purpose, drivers, legal issues, DNR refuse treatment, when, who, making informed decisions, capacity, changes to the ACP, record keeping, who reads it, factors to consider, respecting values and beliefs, those you are unable to fulfil, influence of an ACP, where to find out about ACP	To explain principles and process of advanced care planning (ACP) To list features of the person-centred approach to ACP	303: 1.1 – 1.6 303: 2.1 – 2.10 302: 4.1 301: 6.1 – 6.2 306: 1.3, 4.2 307: 1.4, 3.5	
Lunch				
PM	**ACP (contd.)** Role play and case study	As above	As above	Whole group activity facilitated by the trainer

This example shows how the seven assessed tasks link to the units and assessment criteria, and where they can be found in the learner's portfolio.

Task	Assessed task	Units and assessment criteria			Location & page no.
A	Case study (1)	Unit 301: 5.1 - 5.4	Unit 305: 1.4	Unit 306: 1.1, 1.2, 1.4, 2.1, 2.3; 3.1, 3.2	5–9
B	Mentoring guidance	Unit 301: 3.1 –3.4 4.1 – 4.3	Unit 304 3.1 – 3.3:	Unit 306: 4.5	10 –11
C	Management report	Unit 301: 1.1– 1.3, 6.1– 6.4	Unit 303: 1.1 1.2 2.7 2.10	Unit 306: 1.3,3.3, 3.4, 4.1, 4.4,	12 –23
D	Presentation	Unit 301: 2.1 - 2.4	Unit 305: 2.3, 3.1	Unit 306: 2.2, 4.2, 4.3, 5.1, 5.2	24–29
E	Article	Unit 307: 1.1 –1.4, 2.1 – 2.3			30
F	Case study (2)	Unit 307: 3.1 – 3.5			31–33
G	Guidelines for a new colleague	Unit 303: 1.1 – 1.6 2.1– 2.10, 3.1– 3.5			34–38

3 Planning a short programme

The following example shows a one-day programme aimed at operators of heavy plant equipment. Notice the difference between the morning, based in the classroom, and the afternoon, where the learning takes place outside and the main resource is the actual vehicle.

Course title: Off-highway Truck Maintenance Inspections	**Aim:** For the learner to acquire the knowledge and skills required to complete an operator's inspection of A Manufacturer's X-series off-highway trucks.
Unit: 2: Preparing equipment for work	
Duration: 6 hours	

Time	Session & topic	Teaching method/strategy/differentiation
09.00–09.15	**Registration and induction**: Candidate profiling to determine the extent and currency of skill and knowledge	Learner support; Discussion; Examples
09.15–09.30	**Session 1: safety:** PPE; Personal safety; Equipment safety	Lecture; Slide presentation; Referencing; Activity – flash cards
09.30–09.45	**Session 2: Walk-around inspections:** Isolation; Fluids and oils	Lecture; Slide presentation; Referencing; Activity – pair-wise card set
09.45–10.00	**Operator station and controls:** Identify controls; Test controls	Lecture; Slide presentation; Referencing; Activity – recall
10.00–10.15	**Break**	Available for questions
10.15–10.30	**Summary:** Safety; Walk-around inspections; Operator station/controls	Slide presentation; Discussion
10.30–11.00	**Video: basic safe operation:** Safety; Walk-around Inspection; Operator station & controls; Operator techniques & tips; Machine shutdown	Explaining; Answering questions
11.00–12.00	**Lunch break**	Available for questions
12.00–12.30	**Practical demonstration:** Walk-around inspections; Isolation; Fluids and oils	Demonstrating; Explaining; Answering questions
12.30–13.00	**Practical demonstration:** Operator station and controls; Identify controls; Test controls	Demonstrating; Explaining; Answering questions
13.00–14.00	**Operator practice:** Walk-around inspections; Isolation; Fluids and oils; Operator station and controls; Identify controls; Testing controls	Observing; Questioning; Coaching
14.00–15.00	**Operator test:** Walk-around inspections; Isolation; Fluids and oils; Operator station and controls; Identify controls; Test controls	Observing; Questioning; Coaching
15.00–15.15	**Feedback and evaluation session**	Evaluating

tor/trainer: A Trainer	**Learning objectives:**	
y/time: Thursday, 9.00 a.m.–15.15 p.m.	By the end of the day, the learner will be able to:	
arning centre/venue: Surface Mine Training Centre	• demonstrate appropriate safety procedures	
	• carry out a visual inspection by walking around the vehicle	
	• identify machine operator controls	
	• carry out machine shutdown procedures.	

arner activity	Resources	Assessment
tening; Discussion	Classroom; Paperwork/pens; Laptop/projector	Documentation analysis; Discussion
tening; Observing; Group work	Classroom; Manufacturer's instructions; Laptop/projector	Questionnaire; Feedback to learners; Discussion
tening; Observing; Group work	Classroom; Manufacturer's instructions; Laptop/projector	Oral questions; Professional discussion
tening; Observing; Discussion; eractive game	Classroom; Manufacturer's instructions; Laptop/projector; Laser pointer	Oral questions; Discussion
en discussion; Reflective account	Classroom; Laptop/projector	Open questioning
serving; Asking questions	Laptop/projector/Speakers; Internet; Web-link	Discussion
serving; Asking questions	X-series vehicle that conforms to manufacturer's requirements; Checklist	Questions; Observation
serving; Asking questions	X-series vehicle that conforms to manufacturer's requirements; Checklist	Questions; Observation
monstrating; Explaining	X-series vehicle that conforms to manufacturer's requirements; Checklist	Observation; Feedback to learners
monstrating; Explaining	X-series vehicle that conforms to manufacturer's requirements; Checklist	Feedback to learners
scussion	Record of feedback	Questionnaire

Session planning

Besides creating a scheme of work, you will also need to formally plan individual sessions and keep a record of them. Session plans are your detailed records of how you will use the time available to both you and your learner to achieve the learning objectives. In traditional teaching, session plans often cover given periods of time, but in work-based learning there aren't always set times for learning. If this applies to you, it is your responsibility as the trainer to estimate how much time it will take to run a session and for learners to achieve the learning objectives you set them within that time.

Session plans allow you to go over what you have done with learners and to evaluate the success of each one. It also means you will have a record of what you've done with each learner (or group) and can refer back to previous sessions when recapping or reviewing.

Here are the stages to follow when planning a session:

1 **Set a session aim and SMART learning objectives.**

   First, set an overall aim for your session; then specify exactly what you want your learners to achieve. Your aim can be quite broad, for example, 'to write a report which meets company standards'. Your objectives should be achievable, for example, 'list the headings used in report writing', 'make relevant notes under each heading' and 'compile a two-page report using complete sentences and correct punctuation'. Write the objectives using verbs that relate to the level of learning, for example 'list', 'explain', 'demonstrate', etc.

2 **Break the session down into steps.**

   Now list what you want to teach as a series of smaller steps, for example the different headings used in report writing. At this point, you may find yourself setting more objectives and introducing further sessions because you realise you are trying to cover too much or that you need to introduce another topic. Don't worry; this is all part of the usual planning process.

3 **Choose the delivery methods.**

   Give some thought to the best delivery methods for what you want to teach and the best ways your learners can learn this. Here's where you can think of interesting and imaginative ways to engage learners, for example by using a game or role-play activity. See Chapter 3, 'Delivering learning', on page 63.

4 **Build in assessment for learning.**

   Build in checks for learning after each of your main teaching points, in the form of, say, questions or short activities. They will tell you whether learners have gained the skills and knowledge at a given stage and whether or not they are ready to move on to the next step. See Chapter 4, 'Assessing learning', on page 107.

5 **Sequence the session.**

   Now put the steps and/or activities in order and give them notional timings to fit the time available, for example five or ten minutes. The steps can be in a logical order (particularly if you are teaching something new) or based around various activities. At this stage in your planning, you may find you have to amend some of the steps or change the activities.

6 **Choose and organise resources.**

   You may need equipment or resources to help you with your teaching or to enable your learners to achieve the learning objectives of the session. Make a list of these as you plan each stage of the session.

'A session can be any length of time and still be effective. We work with our workplace trainers to develop sessions that last five minutes as well as those that last one to two hours – or day-long workshops. This supports topics that can be delivered in short bursts or longer sessions – depending on the learner and the time available.'
Training manager

You may need tools, equipment, materials or personal protective equipment if you are planning practical sessions, or marker pens, handouts, laptop or tablet if your teaching involves information, research or knowledge. If you visit different sites or organisations in your job as a trainer, you will have to give some thought to carrying resources around with you and/or liaising with employers about access to resources in the working environment or on their premises.

7 **Evaluate your session.**

Once you have delivered the session, take time to review how it went. For example, ask yourself what went well and what didn't, and what could be improved. Make a note of the changes you would make and incorporate them next time you run the same or a similar session.

Session-plan formats

Here are three examples of session-plan formats. The first one shows a session with an individual learner. The second is an example of a group session from an employability programme. The third shows how to plan from the work task the learner does.

Example 1: Individual session plan

Learner:	Ian MacBeath
Title:	Report writing
Venue and time:	Company training room, 10:30–11:30 p.m.
Aims:	To write a report that meets company standards
Learning objectives:	For Ian to: • list the headings used in report writing • make relevant notes under each heading • compile a two-page report using complete sentences and correct punctuation.

Time	Topic	Method & assessment for learning	Resources
5 mins	Intro & recap Learning objective Recap	Share and agree the learning objectives with Ian Why are we writing this report? Ask Ian to give three reasons linked to his job	Log book *(Only use this as a last resort!)*
10 mins	Headings used in report writing	Ask Ian to add the headings to the preprepared handout	Handout *Remind if necessary*
10 mins	Making notes	Discussion and coaching: Under each heading, discuss what should go into the report. Ian to make notes.	*Coach in note taking as necessary*
10 mins	Turning notes into sentences	Teaching/modelling: Taking one of Ian's notes, show him how to turn these into full sentences to begin each section of the report. Ask him to do the same when he feels confident. Ask him which section he'd like to start with. Suggest the introduction where he outlines what is in the report itself.	Pen & paper Examples of completed fault-finding reports *Check that Ian is happy with the method of going through his notes*

Time	Topic	Method & assessment for learning	Resources
10 mins	Report writing	Ask Ian to have a go at writing his chosen section	
10 mins	Checking	Take turns in error spotting to begin with. When I do it, ask Ian what the error is – go through one or two, then leave Ian to find any more. Allow time for a quick punctuation and/or spelling exercise	Punctuation/ spelling sheets
5 mins	Recap and review	Ask Ian to complete the report before my next visit, with help from his supervisor if necessary. Go over the main points of the session again. Ask Ian what he liked/didn't like about the session and what he would like to achieve next time that is relevant to his job role.	

Give help/ coach as necessary

Use results in next session

Have a word with Laura, Ian's supervisor

Evaluation	Overall, the report writing went really well. Getting Ian to take notes under headings was an effective activity. He immediately grasped the process and wrote his first paragraph using full sentences. He also understood when to begin a new one.
Action	The checking activity didn't work very well because Ian couldn't spot all his mistakes. These were mainly to do with using the possessive apostrophe for plurals and where to put commas.

Preparing for an interview

Tutor	Venue	Course
JW	XYZ Training Centre	Employability – Preparing for an interview

Levels	Date	Time
Level 1	23 June	9:30–11:30 a.m.

Aims of the session

- To introduce learners to the questions likely to be asked by an employer at an interview and to those they can ask

- To enable learners to plan a suitable route to arrive on time

Learning objectives	Assessment
Learners will:	
• identify and compile a list of questions they might be asked at interview	Activity 1
• respond appropriately to questions they might be asked at the interview	
• identify questions to ask which show their interest in the job, placement or course	Activity 2
• plan to arrive at an interview on time by choosing transport and planning a suitable route.	Activity 3

Differentiation	Curriculum references
Use of mind mapping to develop thought process and start written process; tutor-led discussion to develop speaking and listening skills and develop confidence in expressing ideas; pairing up those who have had an interview with those who have not.	This session forms part of a series of three linked to interview skills

Relevant previous knowledge

Use will be made of learners' previous experience of attending interviews.

Time	Content	Learner & trainer activity	Resources and assessment
9:30	Learners to think about interviews they have attended and the types of questions that could be asked	Trainer-led discussion: mind-mapping learners' answers on flipchart Completion of Activity 1 in pairs; questions I might be asked	Whiteboard, marker pens Handout: Activity 1
9:45	Learners to identify questions that the interviewee could ask at the end of an interview	Trainer-led discussion: Individual activity: completion of Activity 2; questions I can ask	Whiteboard, marker pens Handout: Activity 2

Time	Content	Learner & trainer activity	Resources and assessment
10:15	Planning to arrive at the interview on time	Trainer-led discussion on: • modes of transport including the use of timetables • use of online or paper maps • use of satellite navigation • parking considerations and/or walking to the interview venue • arriving early rather than on time. Small-group activity: in twos or threes, learners to use online maps to plan a route using either a car, bus, train or a combination to get to an interview on time	Whiteboard, marker pens Laptops with Internet access Handout: Activity 3
10:50	Introducing learners to the interview evaluation sheet	Trainer to go through the handout and explain how learners can use it to reflect on an interview and to evaluate how well it went	Handout: Interview evaluation sheet
11.30	End of session	Pack away	

- **Health and safety**

  Actively look for hazards; evaluate the risks; report findings if appropriate.

- **Safeguarding**

  Vulnerable adults are people aged 18 years or over who may be unable to take care of themselves, or protect themselves from harm or from being exploited, or who are carers. Provision will be made for this type of learner during the session by ensuring that they identify safe modes of transport and by underlining the need for an accompanying adult.

- **Equality and diversity**

  Use of co-operative learning, previous experiences, differentiated activities, multi-sensory approaches and modelling of processes.

Example 3: Plan for a work-based activity

Here's an example of how to plan a work activity based on what the learner does. This way of planning is useful if you are responsible for individual learners in the workplace and you don't know what you will encounter when you meet them. Planning in this way allows you to build up a bank of sessions and resources to use flexibly, depending on what the learner is currently working on. (You will find further examples of projects that have been planned around work-based activities on pages 88–91.)

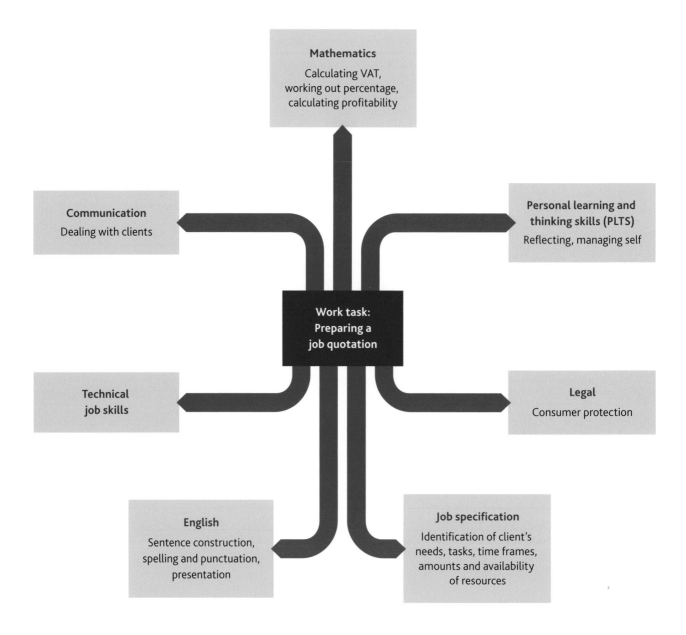

Mathematics
Calculating VAT, working out percentage, calculating profitability

Communication
Dealing with clients

Personal learning and thinking skills (PLTS)
Reflecting, managing self

Work task: Preparing a job quotation

Technical job skills

Legal
Consumer protection

English
Sentence construction, spelling and punctuation, presentation

Job specification
Identification of client's needs, tasks, time frames, amounts and availability of resources

Incorporating English, mathematics and ICT

English, mathematics and ICT are generic skills that all learners need in order to gain employment and perform their jobs effectively. You will come across learners with needs in these areas that you will have to address if they are to make progress and become competent. In some work-based programmes such as apprenticeships, these skills are called functional skills and learners have to achieve separate qualifications in one or more of the following:

- Functional mathematics

- Functional English

- Functional information and communication technologies (ICT)

Learners don't have to be 'doing' English, mathematics or ICT, they just need to integrate them and see their relevance to the job they do, or hope to do. You will find the following principles and examples helpful in making these skills relevant to learners and their jobs.

The principles of effective teaching

Here are some principles for the effective teaching of English, mathematics and ICT linked to the workplace:

- Follow the basic principles of teaching and learning: make sure learners' needs are initially assessed, their learning needs identified, and that the planned programme of teaching and learning is based around each learner's individual needs. Don't map these skills across to the vocational qualification or assume that learners have covered them without teaching them first.

- Induct the learner into the teaching and learning of English, mathematics and/or ICT: make sure they know what will be learning, at what level, and why.

- Don't leave the teaching and acquisition of these skills until the end of learners' programmes. Instead, make sure they are taught right from the start as a formal part of the learner's individual learning programme. Try not to teach them separately, but look for opportunities to embed them in the learner's work tasks whenever possible and use them as your starting point for teaching.

- Embed the skills by identifying the work task that the learner does and use this as your starting point for incorporating aspects of English, mathematics and ICT that are relevant to the job role. (You will find an example of curriculum planning using the work task as your starting point on page 56.)

- When teaching the skills, make sure you make them explicit and relevant to the learner's job. (See the examples below.) Wherever possible, involve the employer in helping to plan relevant projects and in supporting the learner to implement these. Use the planning approach described on page 56, where you start with the work task to embed English, mathematics and ICT into your teaching.

- Make sure you are equipped to teach English, mathematics and/or ICT if they form part of your responsibilities. There are specialist qualifications aimed at teachers of English and mathematics. You might need to update your own skills, perhaps if you are not very confident at using certain aspects of ICT.

- Maintain formal communication between you, the learner, the employer and anyone else involved in teaching, learning and assessing – and keep a record of these. Have a preplanned programme and a range of resources, but aim also to plan as you go based on the individual's needs and any opportunities as they arise.

> **Key term**
>
> **Embedding:** Integrating certain skills within the subject or topic being taught, rather than treating them as separate subjects

'We used to deliver English and maths separately and learners couldn't see the links to their development within their job roles. We then changed our resources and approach to embed English and maths within our vocational delivery and our learners can now see how developing English and maths skills will support their progress and development at work. Our assessors have also found this approach easier when supporting the delivery and achievement of these skills as they can now apply them to job-specific elements of the qualification.'

Training provider

Communicating with colleagues

The following example of good communication between colleagues shows an exchange of emails between an English tutor and a work-based assessor, both responsible for a learner needing to improve his English for his job. It gives you an idea of the benefits for the learner of a close working relationship between them through the amount of detailed information they share to meet the learner's needs.

To: JB   26 March
From: KW

Dawid R

Hi J

Is there anything specific you need me to cover with Dawid tomorrow?

KW

To: KW   26 March
From: JB

Re: Dawid R

Hi K

Yes - there are a few areas he needs to work on in his current assignment. Some of his responses to the tasks need a bit more to fully meet the standards. This is because his English is not always clear. He would benefit by going over each task, checking that he has answered the question using complete sentences, and that his answers make sense as well as checking his spellings.

Specifically, for each task he needs to:

Task 1 – give more details about what he actually did and explain the outcome of the incident (what happened afterwards)

Task 2 – note down what was going on when the accident happened

Task 4 – describe what led to the accident. I think he has a good understanding of what happened but he hasn't quite grasped the causes.

Task 7 – explain how he would contact the first-aider if he had to

Task 8 – explain in detail exactly how he would contact the Emergency Services (what he would use to contact them and where from)

Task 11 – explain in more detail how he would contain an oil spill step by step, making use of some of the items pictured, and explain what he would do with the resulting contaminated waste.

For the next assignment, he can find examples on the Environment Agency website www.environment-agency.gov.uk/news. We had a look at it yesterday so he should be able to do this himself. He should also have a copy of the Environmental Policy. He may struggle with some of the terms used within the tasks. If so, could you pick up on these and let me know how he gets on? I don't want to assess his work before he's ready.

I think his English, written and spoken, is much better than it was and he clearly has a much better understanding than when we started. I was beginning to worry about whether we would be able to get through all the materials but I now think it is achievable.

JB

To: JB   27 March
From: KW

Re:Re: Dawid R

Hi J

Thank you for sending these through. We went through the assignments as you suggested and concentrated on the following:

- Spellings: specifically plurals

- Determiners: A, an and the, when these are used and the rules. This is a huge topic so we shall continue with this after his break

- Verbs and tenses: adding 'ing' - when this is used it's called present continuous (when talking about definite future plans), current situations and likes and dislikes

- We also looked at the spelling when adding 'ing', dropping the e, and adding consonants, etc.

- How to use commas in a list

We need to work on Dawid's speaking and listening next, as he is still not speaking very much. I have given him homework to complete – two e3 reading paper mocks and a written exercise based on the work we have completed today.

I know we should have discussed this at the start, but I have a concern regarding my marking and commenting on his assignments, as I don't want to invalidate his work. I have purposely kept drafts for you to see the improvements he has made with editing his own work. Let me know what you want to do here.

KW

To: KW   27 March
From: JB

Re: Re:Re: Dawid R

Hi K

This is great. We will be able to fix a date for assessment now.

Commenting on Dawid's English is not a problem as long as you don't change his actual answers. I have already seen how he edits his own work. Again, this shouldn't be a problem.

JB

To: JB   27 March
From: KW

Re:Re: Re:Re: Dawid R

Hi J

Just to let you know, Dawid came in to the session much more confident today.

He went to a business meeting with his employer, R, yesterday for the first time and really enjoyed it. We discussed what the meeting was about and he wrote up notes about the purpose of meeting, what was discussed and the outcomes.

It was good to see how much he understood. He said he just listened, which he obviously did. I don't know whether it is possible to mention this to R in your feedback.

He has also started watching more English TV.

One of the things he was struggling with last time was letters and spelling and it has become clear that it is how they are pronounced, particularly a, e, and I. So if you do spell anything for him, could you do this using the sounds of the letters rather than pronouncing the letter itself?

I have also written some sheets based on the standards which we have gone through. I have attached electronic copies for your information but Dawid has the handwritten answers. I thought they might be helpful for evidence of his knowledge and performance.

KW

Embedding English, mathematics and ICT

Here are some examples of ways to embed English, mathematics and ICT. The first example shows how the trainer has adapted an employer's policy into a worksheet for new employees to develop their English and ICT skills. The second example is a reading and comprehension activity used in an employability programme to help learners develop their English. The third example is a project from the waste industries. Here, the trainer obtained data from the employer relating to bin collections and customer complaints and embedded English and mathematics activities within a project on improving customer service.

Example 1

New employee regulations

We expect all our employees to follow these work regulations at all times so that everyone can be safe and enjoy their work. Please complete the chart below to show us that you have understood these. The first one has been done for you.

Our policy says ...	Find an image to illustrate this	Write down one reason why this is important
Be polite and courteous to colleagues and customers at all times.		So that there is a friendly atmosphere at work and we create a professional impression with customers
Come to work well presented, using the clothing we provide, and keep this clean.		
Be on time for work.		
Make sure you are work-ready: • Do not drink alcohol at work or work if you are suffering from a hangover. • Do not take drugs at work or work if you have taken drugs.		
Report any accidents, near-misses or dangerous practices immediately.		
Do not eat while you are working. Eating is restricted to breaks only. Remember at work always to wash your hands before eating.		
No smoking inside the building: smoking is permitted only during breaks in the designated smoking area.		

Example 2

How candidates are selected for interview

How do you think candidates are selected for an interview? Put the following sentences into a sequence of events in the boxes below (you can just use the numbers). The first one has been done for you.

1 Employer phones up or writes to the candidate and asks them to attend an interview/s.

2 Employer notifies the successful candidate by phone followed by an offer letter.

3 Employer receives application forms with CVs and covering letters and date stamps them.

4 Employer shortlists a number of candidates to come in for an interview.

5 Employer reviews the applications against a list of qualifications, skills, attributes required by the job (known as job criteria).

6 Employer usually confirms in writing the date/s, time/s and place/s of the interview.

3

Example 3

Improving customer service

Overview

This assignment will enable you to review your organisation's customer service performance with regard to bin collections, to see if improvements can be made using the data provided.

You'll obtain and identify information, carry out calculations, and present and describe your findings in a report to your manager.

Stage	Relevant to:
1 Read the information	(S1) extract and interpret information from tables, diagrams, charts and graphs
2 Do the calculations	(N1) understand and use whole numbers and understand negative numbers in practical contexts (N2) add, subtract multiply and divide whole numbers using a range of strategies (N5) solve simple problems involving ratio, where one number is a multiple of another (S3) find mean and range
3 Present your findings	(S2) collect and record discrete data and organise and represent information in different ways (S4) use data to assess the likelihood of an outcome

Tips

- Before you start the assignment, talk to your manager or supervisor and plan each stage carefully.

- Keep all your notes, drafts, plans and records of resources and check your work as you go along.

- If possible, get your manager or colleagues to evaluate your performance.

- If in doubt at any time, ask your trainer for guidance.

What you need to do

Stage 1: Read the information

- Read and interpret the information in the two pieces of data provided below. Write a brief introduction for the project and explain what you are going to do, how you might do it and what you might find.

- Decide which calculations you might need to use.

Data

A) Collected bins

MONDAY

Vehicle	Vehicle 1	Vehicle 2	Vehicle 3	Vehicle 4	Vehicle 5	Vehicle 6	Vehicle 7	Vehicle 8	Vehicle 9
Small bin lifts	1232	1131	1121	1068	712	810	1126	1045	1113
Communal bin lifts	11	6	8	7	69	12	9	0	36
Tonnage	17.2	14.15	15.54	16.74	13.82	11.13	14.12	12.59	14.1

TUESDAY

Vehicle	Vehicle 1	Vehicle 2	Vehicle 3	Vehicle 4	Vehicle 5	Vehicle 6	Vehicle 7	Vehicle 8	Vehicle 9
Small bin lifts	1181	1052	857	1156	1024	428	1240	678	1193
Communal bin lifts	3	42	45	11	30	141	12	113	0
Tonnage	15.66	17.15	15.42	17.17	17.16	13.5	16.76	16.21	17.34

WEDNESDAY

Vehicle	Vehicle 1	Vehicle 2	Vehicle 3	Vehicle 4	Vehicle 5	Vehicle 6	Vehicle 7	Vehicle 8	Vehicle 9
Small bin lifts	1058	1099	1183	866	1009	1000	1145	781	1049
Communal bin lifts	1	28	24	55	18	1	16	7	83
Tonnage	14.56	17.93	17.23	15.38	15.59	12.4	16.77	9.99	11.5

THURSDAY

Vehicle	Vehicle 1	Vehicle 2	Vehicle 3	Vehicle 4	Vehicle 5	Vehicle 6	Vehicle 7	Vehicle 8	Vehicle 9
Small bin lifts	1091	1004	794	1112	1060	1022	1146	1254	985
Communal bin lifts	7	30	71	24	28	12	25	8	57
Tonnage	15.25	14.05	14.43	17.57	15.76	16.88	18.97	19.81	16.65

FRIDAY									
Vehicle	Vehicle 1	Vehicle 2	Vehicle 3	Vehicle 4	Vehicle 5	Vehicle 6	Vehicle 7	Vehicle 8	Vehicle 9
Small bin lifts	432	811	444	154	784	964	663	449	470
Communal bin lifts	71	48	124	178	19	11	44	82	83
Tonnage	9.2	11.47	12.61	10.48	11.48	10,50	11.25	10.35	10.75

Note: Communal bins are large bins for flats, nursing homes, schools, etc.

B) Missed bins

January	February	March	April	May	June
428	257	447	184	217	253

July	August	September	October	November	December
246	244	273	315	321	260

Stage 2: Do the calculations

1 Using the collected bins data source, add up the total number of bins collected daily and convert to weekly and monthly figures.

2 Using the collected bins data source, calculate the mean and range of the tonnage/week and the tonnage/month.

3 Using the collected bins data source, find the ratio of the total number of small bin lifts to communal bin lifts. This information should be expressed as the lowest possible ratio.

4 Using the missed bins data source, enter the data on to a spreadsheet and from this produce a graph or chart. Calculate the annual number of missed bins and then work out the percentage of missed bins/month of the annual total.

Stage 3: Present your findings

Prepare a brief report using charts and tables to show your comparisons. Structure your report around the following:

• What you set out to do

• What you found out

• What the data means

• Areas where the data shows that improvements could be made.

The following quotes from trainers show good and bad examples of teaching and embedding English, mathematics and ICT. Which ones do you think exemplify good practice, and why?

'We get employers involved as soon as possible. Our team use a range of work-based projects that they adapt to fit the workplace. They're pretty generic and involve things like carrying out investigations and producing a report which learners present to their work team. As we've been doing it for so long, we've built up expertise and resources so it isn't a big deal for us. Learners love doing the projects. I think this is because they've got the support of their employer as well as us.'

'We mainly train graduates, some of whom lack literacy and numeracy skills at the levels we require. We did buy in specialist online packages, but there was low take-up. I don't think that graduates necessarily see themselves as needing help with these skills, and it didn't help that the actual learning packages were generic and weren't really applicable to the work we do. We've since started using initial assessment at recruitment. We'd expect bespoke resources if we ever went down this route again.'

'Embedding English and mathematics teaching isn't an option for us: we don't have the time or the expertise so we contract out. The problem is continuity – the tutor gets one hour a week with the learner, comes in with her curriculum and delivers it. She sometimes talks to the employer, but she doesn't have any formal contact with other staff as we contract our assessment and off-job training out too.'

'We deal with many learners who have particular needs. We already know that most come to us wanting help with their literacy, numeracy and ICT to get them into employment. We make a point of front-loading any teaching so that they start getting the support they need based around a thorough initial assessment. We also make sure that each learner has an individual profile and we structure our teaching and learning around this. Potential employers get to see the progress they've made when we conduct interviews. For most of our learners, it's their first big achievement.'

'We're involved in offender learning. Most have to earn the privilege of getting on to a teaching programme through good behaviour. By the time they've got to this stage, motivation isn't a problem as they know they'll improve their job prospects if they get a qualification.'

'I teach ICT and have difficulties trying to make the teaching relevant to my work-based learners. I get mixed groups and in some areas like Early Years there aren't many opportunities for ICT. If you combine that with learners who don't see the relevance to their jobs, you've got a real problem keeping them motivated.'

The minimum core

If you are working towards a teaching qualification – and even if you are not – you will be required to demonstrate your own skills of literacy, language, numeracy and information and communication technology (ICT) to at least level 2. This is known as the 'minimum core' and you need it to be able to support your learners with their skills of English, mathematics and ICT. It will also enable you to teach your area of specialism as effectively as possible.

Here are some examples of how you can demonstrate using the minimum core when planning learning.

Remember

The minimum core applies to *all* parts of the trainer's role, including delivering and assessment of learning.

Literacy	Language	Numeracy	ICT
Reading the qualification handbook and making notes on what you will deliver and assess	Asking questions to find out a learner's prior knowledge and experience, and listening to their responses	Working out how many sessions and hours will be required in a scheme of work	Using a word processor or other application to create handouts and resources
Reading relevant internal and external guidance to learn the requirements for initial and diagnostic assessment	Talking to others involved with the learners' progress, listening to questions and answering them appropriately	Planning how long various teaching, learning and assessment activities will take during a session	Using email or social networking to communicate appropriately
Completing templates and forms and checking spelling, grammar and punctuation	Speaking to learners about their individual needs and discussing how they can be supported	Calculating how long initial and diagnostic assessment activities will take, and the time it will take to ascertain and interpret the results	Using new technology to support particular learning needs
			Preparing visual presentations or online materials and uploading them to a virtual learning environment (VLE) or other accessible system

Links to the teaching qualifications

Level 3 Award in Education and Training
Unit title: *Understanding and using inclusive approaches in education and training*

Learning outcomes	Assessment criteria
1 Understand inclusive teaching and learning approaches in education and training	**1.1** Describe features of inclusive teaching and learning
	1.2 Compare the strengths and limitations of teaching and learning approaches used in own area of specialism in relation to meeting individual learner needs
	1.3 Explain why it is important to provide opportunities for learners to develop their English, mathematics, ICT and wider skills
2 Understand ways to create an inclusive teaching and learning environment	**2.1** Explain why it is important to create an inclusive teaching and learning environment
	2.2 Explain why it is important to select teaching and learning approaches, resources and assessment methods to meet individual learner needs
	2.3 Explain ways to engage and motivate learners
	2.4 Summarise ways to establish ground rules with learners
3 Be able to plan inclusive teaching and learning	**3.1** Devise an inclusive teaching and learning plan
	3.2 Justify own selection of teaching and learning approaches, resources and assessment methods in relation to meeting individual learner needs
4 Be able to deliver inclusive teaching and learning	**4.1** Use teaching and learning approaches, resources and assessment methods to meet individual learner needs
	4.2 Communicate with learners in ways that meet their individual needs
	4.3 Provide constructive feedback to learners to meet their individual needs

Please note: 2.4 and 4.3 are covered in Chapter 3, 'Delivering learning'.

Level 4 Certificate in Education and Training
Unit title: *Planning to meet the needs of learners in education and training*

Learning outcomes	Assessment criteria
1 Be able to use initial and diagnostic assessment to agree individual learning goals with learners	**1.1** Analyse the role and use of initial and diagnostic assessment in agreeing individual learning goals
	1.2 Use methods of initial and diagnostic assessment to negotiate and agree individual learning goals with learners
	1.3 Record learners' individual learning goals
2 Be able to plan inclusive teaching and learning in accordance with internal and external requirements	**2.1** Devise a scheme of work in accordance with internal and external requirements
	2.2 Design teaching and learning plans which meet the aims and individual learning needs of all learners and curriculum requirements
	2.3 Explain how own planning meets the individual needs of learners
	2.4 Explain ways in which teaching and learning plans can be adapted to meet the individual needs of learners
	2.5 Identify opportunities for learners to provide feedback to inform inclusive practice
3 Be able to implement the minimum core in planning inclusive teaching and learning	**3.1** Analyse ways in which minimum core elements can be demonstrated in planning inclusive teaching and learning
	3.2 Apply minimum core elements in planning inclusive teaching and learning
4 Be able to evaluate own practice when planning inclusive teaching and learning	**4.1** Review the effectiveness of own practice when planning to meet the individual needs of learners, taking account of the views of learners and others
	4.2 Identify areas for improvement in own planning to meet the individual needs of learners

3 Delivering learning

There are many ways of delivering training sessions and encouraging learning, but some methods are better than others at getting learners to think or do things for themselves, and some are more appropriate to the workplace than others. When you deliver learning you will use a variety of approaches because they develop different skills in your learners.

Whether you work with learners one to one or in groups, your starting point for delivering learning should always be the individual learner. This means finding out what motivates that learner and how to identify and meet their individual needs. Therefore before you decide how to deliver learning, you will need to take account of:

- what motivates your learners

- your learners' learning preferences

- inclusive approaches to teaching and training

- your vocational specialism.

This chapter introduces the main teaching methods to use in the workplace, the workshop and the training room, and gives practical advice on how to choose the right methods for the topics you teach and for your learners. You will also find out how to choose and use the most relevant resources for each method, including digital technologies.

Learners as individuals

All your learners are unique individuals with different motivations and learning preferences, and so it is vital that you get to know each one as a person in order to decide how best to work with them.

Your learners will have different reasons for learning – some positive, some negative. Either way, their motivation – what drives them to learn in the first place – will affect their approach to learning. Knowing what motivates your learners can help you plan and deliver learning that is relevant, likely to engage and encourage them, and will help them accomplish their tasks and learning objectives.

Activity: Getting to know your learners

Read the following statements by learners and assess who you think will be the most and who the least likely to achieve success on their course. Then consider the reasons for this.

Is the learner likely to succeed?	Yes	No
1 'I need to get a job. That's why I have started this back-to-work course.'	☐	☐
2 'The only qualifications I've got are the ones I left school with. Doing this traineeship is the beginning for me. I want to get on a plumbing apprenticeship.'	☐	☐
3 'I want to do the accounts for my dad's business, so this electronic bookkeeping course is the solution.'	☐	☐
4 'I got a grade D for my GCSE maths. You have to get a C or above to get on an apprenticeship, so that's why I'm redoing my GCSE.'	☐	☐
5 'All employees have to undergo basic health and safety training – that's why I'm here. I'd probably have an accident if I wasn't!'	☐	☐
6 'I got this Saturday job in my local salon because I've always wanted to be a hairdresser.'	☐	☐
7 'The business I work for is relocating to France in six months' time. I've known about this for ages so I need to learn the language – now!'	☐	☐
8 'My partner bought me a place on this car maintenance class and I was horrified. I can see the benefits now I've been coming for three weeks and I think I'll carry on.'	☐	☐
9 'I knew that if I didn't learn how to use social media I wouldn't get promoted.'	☐	☐
10 'I hate reading and writing. I've never been good at them, and now my employer says everyone has to get a level 2 qualification as a condition of employment.'	☐	☐

Numbers 1, 3 and 6 are statements by learners who are motivated to learn for its own sake or because they really want to do it. The other statements are from learners with negative reasons or with conditions imposed on them for needing to learn.

Usually, learners who have their own, positive reasons for wanting to learn – who are intrinsically motivated – are more likely to succeed and to retain what they have learned than those who have external factors imposed on them that mean they have to do something (extrinsic motivation). Learners in the workplace are often a mixture of both, depending on whether their reason for learning is mainly a requirement by their employer (extrinsic) or mainly because they want to learn for themselves (intrinsic).

Key terms

Intrinsic motivation: Those who are intrinsically motivated will have their own internal reasons for wanting to learn

Extrinsic motivation: Those who are extrinsically motivated will have their reasons for learning imposed upon them by other people, or due to needs or circumstances

Improving motivation

As a trainer, you are likely to have to deal with learners who have negative as well as positive motivation. There is no magic switch for turning people on to learning: they may be on your programme because they have to be there and will need you to help motivate them.

There are things you can do to improve and maintain motivation when you are training. The following table lists some situations where you may encounter poor or flagging motivation, the reasons for it and what you can do about it.

Situation	Reason	Remedy
Your learners start to show signs of bad behaviour.	They are bored, or your training methods don't suit the topic or ignore the different ways of tackling it.	Try varying the pace, your methods and approaches to delivery.
A learner is disengaged from learning.	They don't see the relevance of what you're doing.	Find out what interests them and use this as a focus for learning.
A learner who has previously done well now seems to be falling behind.	They have a personal problem.	Find out what the problem is and set aside time to help them catch up.
Some learners seem bored or disengaged.	They aren't being challenged enough (or, conversely, the level of challenge is too high)	Make sure you know exactly where each individual is in terms of their progress, and set extension activities to keep them busy or to meet their particular needs.
	They have behavioural problems.	Take them to one side, discuss their behaviour and be clear about what needs to change and why. Ask for help or refer them for specialist help if the problem is beyond your expertise.
One learner is dominating the group.	They want to impress you or their peers.	Name those you would like to answer or contribute.
	They may be insecure about their learning.	Ignore inappropriate contributions and reward appropriate behaviour (for example, when they complete a task or take their turn).
Some learners don't finish their work on time.	The work is too hard.	Set them something you know they can achieve, giving plenty of encouragement.
	They are distracted by others in the group.	Ask them to move places to sit next to/work with a different learner.
	The employer is not committed to their learning programme.	Talk to the employer directly and gain his or her commitment; set activities directly relevant to the business and the learner's job role.

For more information on delivery methods, see page 74.

'I had a learner who had already done a Level 3 Business Administration qualification, so thought she should be doing a Level 4 NVQ. Through the initial conversation with her, it became obvious that her job role was actually aligned to Level 3. When I dug a bit deeper, I found she had only completed two units within the Level 3 qualification and that these were at Level 2. Her motivation was wanting to progress to a high-level PA job but feedback about her performance from her employer confirmed that she needed development to perform effectively within her existing role. Maintaining her motivation was definitely a challenge – what she needed was a reality check!'

Trainer

Key terms

Extension activities: Extra activities designed to challenge learners further

Level: A measure of the demand of a unit, qualification or activity; the higher the level, the more demanding it is

Identifying 'What's in it for me (WIFM)?'

Another good way to look at learner motivation is to identify 'what's in it for me?' for the learner. Getting learners to identify the benefits of the learning for themselves (the WIFM) is often a good way to motivate them to learn. Learners are not always motivated by the same things that drive you, their trainer, or by learning for its own sake, but they might be motivated by what's in it for them. So a WIFM regarding 'planning a budget' may be that the learner will be able to manage their own money better with the new skill.

The long-term benefits of WIFM for learners include:

- an ability to put theory into practice – for example, learning how to deal with a customer by role-playing activities off the job, then dealing with a real customer on the job

- the chance to work alongside employees and develop skills such as teamwork, communication and time management

- an appreciation of what an employer is looking for in an employee, such as reliability, personal presentation, manners and punctuality

- improving skills such as English, maths and ICT and working towards qualifications

- the possibility of a permanent position, a promotion or a pay rise.

Initial and diagnostic assessment

Initial and diagnostic assessment happens at the beginning of a learning programme. It is helpful to think of initial assessment as a process that helps you gain an overall picture of the learner, their previous achievements, what they are capable of and what they hope to accomplish. Diagnostic assessment helps to identify specific learner strengths and needs. Identifying learner needs is the starting point for finding out what motivates learners to learn, what their potential might be and what their learning needs are in relation to the vocational area you plan to teach.

Initial and diagnostic assessment of learners might involve finding out about:

- their occupational suitability for the job role

- their expectations of the job role and the training

- their existing skills, knowledge and experience

- their basic skills – literacy, numeracy; mathematics; English; ICT

- their personal skills such as teamworking, problem-solving and communication

- their learning support needs and learning preferences.

Remember

The results of initial and diagnostic assessment should be shared with all those involved in delivering the learning.

For workplace learners, an important consideration is the learner's job role, particularly if learners are working towards standards or qualifications at levels 3 or 4. Qualifications at higher levels require learners to take on particular responsibilities (such as supervising other staff) or to acquire technical skills that require access to certain equipment, and/or the opportunity to acquire and demonstrate these under certain conditions.

'We carry out a training needs analysis at the start to identify any gaps in provision. This forms the basis for discussion with the employer so that extra responsibility can be given to the learner or a project can be set if necessary. We also get our learners to fill in an "experience record" describing their responsibilities in detail – an essential starting point for us to understand their job role.'

Training provider

If you are the person responsible for carrying out initial assessment, you will need to find out what type of assessments or tests you are expected to use, and how to interpret and use the results. If someone else is doing the initial assessments, you should expect to be given the results before meeting your learners, because they tell you where your learners' starting points are. It's pointless planning learning that's at the wrong level, or not relevant to your learner or their job. You need to pitch the training at the level of the learner and enable them to progress at a steady pace by gradually increasing the extent of the challenge. Initial assessment can also be used at the beginning of a new job task, or unit of a qualification, as your learner progresses through their training programme.

'We've introduced initial assessment within the resources we use with learners. At the start of each workbook, we ask learners to self-assess against the topics they contain and to say if they know the topic well, need some support or don't know it at all. This helps them identify the sections of the workbook to focus on, they discuss it with their work-based assessor, then develop a learning plan for tackling the workbook.'

Training manager

> **Key point**
>
> You will find help with designing a robust system of initial assessment in Read, H., *The best initial assessment guide (2013)*.

'The reality is you don't always get the luxury of initial assessment when dealing with groups of workplace learners – especially if you are a subcontractor. The first time I meet my learners is in a mixed group of 20 or so and I have to carry out my own assessments to tell me where they are and plan from there.'

Freelance trainer

Understanding learning preferences

Finding out how learners prefer to learn does not, by itself, help you plan or manage their learning. Research shows that many models of 'learning styles' are in use, but that not all of them are based on valid or reliable information.[10]

Here are some tips:

- **Don't rely on a 'learning preferences' model.** Think, instead, in terms of starting an ongoing discussion with each learner about the best ways they think they learn or approach different tasks. For example, some learners prefer to learn by doing a task for themselves, others by observing someone else, or by asking questions or reading. You can then follow up the initial conversation each time you review the learner's progress.

10 Coffield, F. et al. (2004), *Learning Styles for Post-16 Learners: What do we know?* (LSRC)

- **Avoid labelling learners according to their preferred learning style.** It's easy to say, for example, 'She's an activist – she likes learning by doing' or 'He likes reading and studying, so he's a theorist', and thereby categorise the learner. The best learners are those who can adapt their ways of learning to the circumstances, so encourage learners to try out new ways of doing things, even if it means that they make mistakes (as long as it's safe to do so).

- **Be clear about the purpose of initially assessing learning styles or preferences.** Ask, 'Why are we doing this?' and 'What will we do with the results?' Don't raise learners' expectations that they have a choice unless you have the resources to support them and unless you intend to act on what each learner says.

- **Use the type of learning as your main pointer to methods of delivery and/or assessment.** For example, skills-based training will mean hands-on delivery methods and observing learners to ensure that learning has taken place. (See page 74 for more information.)

> ### Remember
>
> The way *you* prefer to learn is not the way you will teach your learners. Instead, you should use a variety of methods to suit both learners and the domain of learning within which you are setting your learning objectives.

Activity: How do you like to learn?

Tick the methods you love and the ones you hate:

Learning method	Yes, I love to learn like this	No, I'd never choose this method
Trying things out for myself	☐	☐
Writing and making notes	☐	☐
Being shown what to do	☐	☐
Talking things over with others	☐	☐
Watching someone else and copying them, either directly or by viewing videos or webinars	☐	☐
Reading books, journals or magazines	☐	☐
Listening to someone speak (lectures, digital podcasts or radio, CDs and audio)	☐	☐
Using e-methods: the Internet or e-learning	☐	☐
Learning in a group	☐	☐
Understanding why the topic is important and its relevance to me	☐	☐
Making mistakes	☐	☐

What do your answers tell you? Do you like to learn in one or two ways, or do you have a range of preferences? Think about these methods in relation to your learners, and see whether you can identify ways of varying your delivery to take account of these.

You might also like to use this activity with your learners.

Learning by experience

A further consideration is that work-based learners will be learning through experience at work. David Kolb (1984)[11] developed a model of how people learn from experience, which can be applied to workplace learning. He based the model on the ideas of Kurt Lewin, who theorised that people learn through their experiences. Lewin thought that people form abstract ideas from reflecting on their experiences and that they then test these ideas and concepts in new situations, leading to further experiences and reflection. Kolb turned this model into a diagram he called 'The experiential learning cycle', shown here.

The learner learns by...

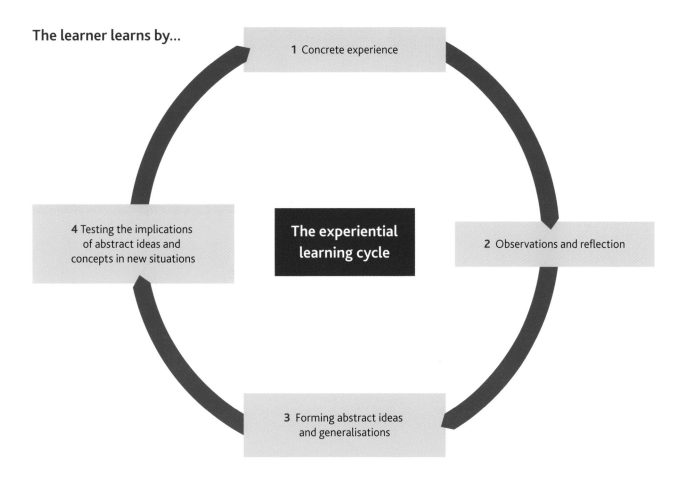

1 Concrete experience

2 Observations and reflection

3 Forming abstract ideas and generalisations

4 Testing the implications of abstract ideas and concepts in new situations

The experiential learning cycle

You don't have to treat the cycle as a series of steps that must be followed every time. Kolb believed that you can start learning at any point on the cycle. Learners may have to go around the cycle several times to develop understanding, particularly when working at higher levels, for example when diagnosing faults, applying skills that require total accuracy, solving complex problems or arriving at professional judgements.

Inclusive practice and the law

The Equality Act became law in 2010, replacing the previous acts and regulations that formed the basis of anti-discrimination law in Great Britain. The legislation requires equal treatment of everyone who is accessing employment as well as private and public services – such as access to government-funded vocational provision.

> **Key term**
>
> **Inclusive practice:** Making sure all learners are given opportunities to take part in learning and that they are not excluded

---

11 Kolb, D. (1984), *Experiential Learning as the Science of Learning and Development.* Englewood Cliffs, NJ: Prentice Hall.

The nine 'protected characteristics' within the Act relate to:

- age

- disability

- gender

- gender reassignment

- marriage and civil partnership

- race

- religion or belief

- sexual orientation

- pregnancy and maternity.

The law requires organisations and everyone working in them to take a proactive stance in promoting equality and seeking to avoid unlawful discrimination before it occurs. There are seven different types of discrimination:

1 **Associative discrimination:** direct discrimination against someone because they are associated with another person with a protected characteristic.

2 **Direct discrimination:** discrimination because of a protected characteristic.

3 **Indirect discrimination:** when a rule or policy that applies to everyone can disadvantage a person with a protected characteristic.

4 **Discrimination by perception:** direct discrimination against someone because others think they have a protected characteristic.

5 **Harassment:** behaviour deemed offensive by the recipient.

6 **Harassment by a third party:** the harassment of staff or others by people not directly employed by an organisation, such as an external consultant or visitor.

7 **Victimisation:** discrimination against someone because they made or supported a complaint under equality legislation.

Activity: Looking at diversity

Take a minute or two to think of some of the learners you are working with.
Now answer the following questions.

How many of your learners:	Answer
• don't speak English at home?	
• come from another country?	
• have a disability?	
• have a specific learning difficulty?	
• are older learners?	
• have no recognised qualifications?	
• come from rural or isolated backgrounds?	
• are school leavers?	
• have other factors that affect their learning? (Note what these are.)	

In the answers you gave above, you probably have more than one learner in several of the categories in addition to the last two. Look at the spread of your answers. Which categories do they mainly fall into? Are they young or old? Are they from different countries? Is English their second language?

You will know from your answers that there is no such thing as a 'typical' learner. Each one is unique, and so each group or individual you teach will be different. This means that every time you have a training session you will need to create an environment where each learner feels included and is able to make a worthwhile contribution, whatever their circumstances and abilities.

Creating a group profile

When working with a group of learners, you might find it helpful to create a 'group profile'. This will act as a visual reminder to help you understand more about each individual. For example, if you have a group of 12 learners working towards a beauty therapy qualification, you can break this information down to enable you to give appropriate support as your session progresses. The information should be used to differentiate your activities to suit your learners and to support any particular needs.

A group profile can include information on each learner's:

- name, age, ethnicity and gender
- prior skills, knowledge, experience and qualifications
- initial and diagnostic assessment results
- learning preferences
- learning needs and support requirements
- barriers, challenges, health or personal issues that might affect learning
- attendance, behaviour and motivation concerns, with support strategies
- individual targets and additional targets to stretch and challenge learning further.

> ### Key terms
>
> **Differentiation:** How trainers adjust their training methods and tailor their resources to meet the individual needs, aptitudes and interests of learners
>
> **Group profile:** Information about each individual learner in a group that will help support their learning

Producing a detailed group profile is a good way to get to know your learners as individuals. Having your group profile as a separate document will save you repeating the information on each session plan if you have the same learners regularly. The information on the group profile should not be shared with other learners, but should be shared with any colleagues who are in contact with your learners, to ensure consistency of support.

Differentiating within groups

You should incorporate differentiation at the planning stage. For each key activity you want your learners to complete, ask yourself two questions:

- 'How can I challenge the most able learners – the ones that know what they are doing and who always finish first?'

- 'What do I need to put in place to help less able learners?'

Practical strategies

Here are some practical suggestions for differentiation when teaching a group.

- **Offer extra activities**

  Devise extra extension activities (for knowledge) or skills tasks that can be included in each session to be used by more able learners. For example:

  - ask them to buddy up with another learner and ask or answer questions throughout the session, as appropriate

  - have a bank of resources containing more challenging questions and activities for stronger learners to choose from

  - ask the learners to produce a verbal, written or visual summary of the key points of the session

  - get them to move on to the next step on their own: ask 'What would you do next?' or set 'What if …?' scenarios to check and broaden their knowledge.

- **Challenge learners when needed**

  Challenge the learner who says, 'I've done this before' or 'I know this already.' They may mean 'I'm bored' or 'I don't want to do this.' Ask them to show you that they can still do the task, or to choose something they haven't done before, or redesign the activity so that it is more challenging instead.

- **Take care with resource design**

  Think about how you design your resources – for learners with dyslexia or who are visually impaired, you will need to use an easy-to-read font such as Century Gothic in a bigger size than usual – at least 14 point – on handouts and other materials. If possible, paper should be not be white: cream, pale yellow or blue are better. Alternatively, the learner could use a coloured plastic wallet in which to place handouts before reading them. You can also adapt the background to slides on a screen so it is not white.

- **Use visual aids**

  When you present information, incorporate a visual reminder for those who struggle to process information – an infographic or a series of images illustrating each key point.

- **Give learners options**

  Identify opportunities for learners to choose what they do. For example, have a number of workstations around the room with different activities, so that learners can move around during the session and choose different options. You might offer a workshop session with a variety of practice exercises to choose from; choices about how to take notes when carrying out group work; or choices about what to focus on during a revision session. Encourage learners to develop their skills through their choices, providing they are relevant.

Key term

Infographic: A way of representing information graphically and visually, using pictures as well as words

- **Vary learner pairings**

  If you work with groups of learners, ask individuals to work together in pairs, and vary the pairings. Don't keep pairing an able learner with a less able one, as this can be frustrating to both. Often, two evenly matched learners will work at the same pace.

- **Use specialist help**

  Working one to one with learners who have particular needs may mean asking for specialist help. Don't be afraid to ask; there should be other staff with the expertise to help you and your learners.

Maintaining motivation

To maintain motivation overall, make sure that you do the following during a group session:

Reassure learners	Make it clear from the beginning that you are aware that some learners know or can do more than others, as this will reassure everyone.
Vary the pace of the session	Consider a change of pace at various points during the session. Have a few prepared questions you can quickly use, then set some quiet time for reading. Set some questions mid-session and target them at individuals to check their understanding. Using open questions, that is, those that start with *who, what, when, where, why* and how are good at gaining responses. (Closed questions are those that only gain a 'yes' or 'no' answer, which doesn't really tell you what your learner understands.) Have a mixture of questions, some to build the confidence of less able learners and others to challenge the more able.
Use incentives and rewards	Giving out rewards are good 'one-off' incentives (you can reward effort on the part of slower learners too). Examples of rewards can include verbal praise, 'points' that can be built up over time to be exchanged for items such as pens or books, or allowing learners to leave a few minutes early, if it's acceptable for them to do so.
Mix up abilities	If you're going to use group activities, make sure you allocate roles and tasks in advance that take account of both slower and stronger learners. Aim for a good mix of abilities – and personalities.

'Many of our learners work on farms. A lot of the time they are driving around in a tractor working on their own, which makes it difficult for them to interact with other learners. We make a point of using collaborative learning during off-job training. This is a theme that runs through all our teaching and learning. We run a residential week early on in their programme so that they get to know one another and they take part in team activities. We introduce them to assignments and get them to buddy up in pairs or threes. They each take responsibility for a particular aspect of the work and they use laptops and the college's virtual learning environment (VLE) to contact each other. We bring them in for two days at a time so that they can work together to finish their assignments, and they present their work to the whole group.'

Trainer, land-based college

It's important to identify *all* the factors that affect learners' motivation and access to learning. As we have seen, this means thinking of each learner as an individual with a unique set of circumstances and needs that they bring to their learning.

Recognising diversity among learners can help trainers reduce barriers. These barriers can be to do with the learners themselves – including learners with disabilities – or with your own attitudes, beliefs, organisational culture or practical issues.

All learners will benefit if you take a proactive stance on inclusivity in your training, as the following examples from trainers show:

'When we were reviewing the way in which we described diagrams to one of our learners who has a visual impairment, it became apparent that other learners preferred to listen to what was on the page too – and that they remembered much more in this way. It worked particularly well for our learners at higher levels where they had lots of information to absorb. We now incorporate auditory methods as part of our delivery for all learners.'

'We've had learners who don't cope well in groups because of the noise or "sensory overload". This taught me the importance of "quiet time". For example, I start off with a quiet activity – like reading or researching. I put it on screen and learners come in and get on with it. If anyone's boisterous, late, or asking "What are we doing, then?" it's usually the others who shush them and point to the screen.'

'I had two learners who were hearing-impaired and who didn't want the rest of the group to know, so the first time I taught them I spread a range of materials across the table in the front. Others avoided this table when they came in because it looked occupied, leaving it free for these two learners.'

'I make a point of finding out how learners with dyslexia prefer to be supported. They may prefer a particular colour of paper to read from, so you have to use this when designing presentation slides or handouts. Also, I tell learners at the beginning how to access slides and notes so that I'm not expecting them to listen and write at the same time.'

Choosing the right delivery method

For your learners to be successful, you need to choose the right strategy for how you are going to train them. When making your choice, you need to consider the following aspects of a particular session.

1 **The number of learners**

   Are you training an individual, a large group of perhaps 15 or more or a small group? The number of learners you teach has a huge impact on time and resources; for example, you would find it difficult to coach individually in a large group because it would take too long and you could only give your attention to one learner at a time.

2 **The subject matter and learning objectives**

   What are the learning objectives, and how best will you get learners to achieve them? Here's where the learning domains and taxonomies or hierarchies of learning come in (see page 34). You need to be clear about what you want learners to achieve: for example, a demonstration will enable the learner to see a whole task from beginning to end and understand what's involved, but they won't be able to do it for themselves unless you make time for this as well.

Remember

Your work-based learners will be learning through experience at work. With this in mind, you may find it helpful to link your choice of delivery methods to the experiential learning cycle on page 69.

3 **Your learners' individual needs and preferences**

Where is each individual learner in relation to your learning objectives?
When choosing your method, you will need to take account of the
fact that learners don't all learn in the same way and at the same pace.
For information on meeting learners' individual needs and learning
preferences, see page 64.

4 **The level of learner involvement**

Another important consideration is how much your chosen delivery
method will involve the learner. Strategies that involve you doing a lot
of the work don't always require very much of learners. For example, you
might think you've covered a topic by giving a skills' demonstration, but
your learners have only watched you, and might have learned little or
nothing. Never be afraid to recap and repeat things. It's probably the first
time your learner has heard or seen something and they may need time
and reinforcement to take it in.

5 **Relevance to the workplace**

With workplace learners you need to remember that they are learning from
carrying out the job itself and from their colleagues, as well as from you.
With this in mind, you won't always be 'delivering' directly to learners:
instead, think in terms of adopting methods to support, hone or improve
performance and which help to make their learning clear to them. They
need to know what they are doing and understand why they are doing it.

6 **Sector-specific constraints**

Your choice of delivery method may need to take account of legal or
resource constraints in your vocational sector. For example, there will be
health and safety issues to consider when dealing with gas or electricity,
or heavy plant equipment, and infection control to consider within care.
For skills training there will be the cost of resources to consider. You
must identify these for your specialist area and comply with them when
choosing the best methods of delivering learning.

The main delivery methods

The table below shows the main delivery methods, how to use them, the area of learning involved, and which of the methods involve learners (active methods).

Method	When to use it	Area of learning (domain)	Active for the learner?
Demonstration and instruction	For a step-by-step task breakdown: showing how it should be done at the beginning of a programme or session	Doing (psychomotor)	✗
Presentation and lecture	For presenting and explaining knowledge and ideas	Knowledge and attitude (cognitive and affective)	✗
Workplace coaching (one to one)	For improving individual performance	Doing	✔
Facilitation of group work and discussion	For involving learners: discussion is good for exploring issues For higher-order cognitive skills like analysis and synthesis of theories and ideas	Attitude, knowledge (affective and cognitive)	✔
Games and activities	For changing topics or shifting the pace in a session – or just for fun.	Knowledge, attitude and doing	✔
Role play	For enabling learners to try out new skills and behaviours in a safe environment, for example dealing with complaints or conflict	Attitude and doing	✔
Simulation	For practising skills, performance and procedures in a safe environment	Doing	✔
Written and practical projects and assignments	For putting knowledge and/or skills into practice	Knowledge and doing	✔
Self-directed learning	For self-study or e-learning modules; for carrying out library or Internet research; or for designing a project with the learner that they carry out themselves	Knowledge, attitude and doing	✔

Trainers are often encouraged to use active methods, but it's a myth to assume that these are always the best methods to use. Successful teaching and learning involve using a variety of different strategies in combination with one another. For example, the way in which you introduce learners to new skills, knowledge and ideas can mean starting off with a demonstration (a passive method) and following this with active methods such as practice and coaching.

Activity: Which method for which learner?

Use the following checklist to gauge how prepared your learners are for you to use methods that involve them taking responsibility for their own learning. For each learner, choose the method that most closely describes the stage they have reached, then read the suggested answers below for ways of working with them.

This learner is ...	Method
1 dependent on me to direct their learning and to determine how I teach them for most of the time.	
2 interested in their own learning: they make suggestions and want to try other ways of doing things.	
3 involved in their own learning: they treat me as an equal; I mainly facilitate their learning.	
4 self-motivated and self-directed: they only refer to me when they need me.	

Suggested answers

1   If your learner is new to the area of learning, use trainer-centred methods like demonstration and instruction until they are confident about applying what they have learned. Then move to more self-directed methods: for example, start by negotiating a coaching session with them based on what they think they need to do next; or ask them to choose an area they would like to improve and agree some learning objectives for the learner to achieve.

2   This learner is engaged in their own learning. Encourage them to take more ownership by trying out different methods and encourage them to reflect on the impact and effectiveness of these different methods on their learning. (See Chapter 5 for more on this.)

3   Negotiate learning objectives with this kind of learner. You can take a coaching and project-based approach to improve knowledge and performance as necessary.

4   This learner is capable of choosing their own methods of learning. All you have to do is keep them on target. Make sure you are available to offer support and encouragement, though, particularly if you are training groups of learners.

Workplace coaching

Coaching is a one-to-one delivery method best used when you are working with learners in the workplace, where they need to develop specific skills and/or improve their performance. You can coach small groups, but because coaching is fairly intensive you'll find there's a limit to what you can achieve – unless you're teaching a team activity such as a sport – because you won't have time to coach everyone individually in one session.

It is helpful to think of coaching as a way of improving learning and encouraging expertise. This makes it an ideal method for the workplace, where your aim is to improve a learner's performance on the job.

Coaching versus mentoring

Vocational training usually involves coaching rather than mentoring. Learners learn *with* a coach alongside them. Coaching involves the learner achieving particular learning objectives that they negotiate with their coach as they go. The aim is for the coachee to learn new skills or improve their performance, usually within a structured programme of coaching. This could be via a process of negotiated learning objectives; or it could be where the coachee has to achieve preset levels of performance.

Learners usually learn *from* a mentor. A mentor is an experienced or more senior person who takes responsibility for the progress of someone with less experience. In the workplace, this could mean appointing an experienced employee to oversee the work of an apprentice. Mentors don't always teach or train their mentees, although they may give advice, observe or ask them to reflect upon a task. For example, they may give particular career advice or help a new employee find their way around the company and negotiate organisational politics.

Instruction versus coaching

Think of coaching and instruction as different styles of delivery at opposite ends of the spectrum. Coaching involves a learner doing a task or learning with the trainer alongside for support, whereas instruction involves the trainer telling and/or showing the learner how to do something.

When teaching learners how to do something new, you will use a mixture of instruction and coaching. When planning, keep in mind the key differences between the two methods:

Instruction is about:

- telling or showing the learner something in a formal way

- passing on your knowledge or skill to your learner

- demonstrating skills or tasks that are new to your learner (for example, new procedures, activities, sequencing and accompanying procedural knowledge that they are meeting for the first time).

Coaching is about:

- the learner taking responsibility for their own learning

- you actively encouraging the learner

- questioning the learner

- giving feedback

- building on the learner's existing skills or knowledge

- helping the learner develop high-order skills (such as evaluating their own performance, solving problems, and suggesting and trying out different options for themselves).

Increasing challenge in knowledge and thinking

For coaching to be effective, you need to plan each session in advance so that you are prepared for the individual learner and their learning needs. You should be agreeing more challenging learning objectives with them at each stage, based on what the learner demonstrates they can do, and providing ongoing feedback on their progress and performance to inform these objectives.

One way of increasing challenge is to use structured questioning. This is where you ask the learner questions about what they are doing and why, and how well they think they are doing it at each stage of a task.

Here are some examples of questions that demand progressively more of the learner:

- Memory or recall: *What are the bones in the leg called?*

- Observation: *What happened when you kicked the ball with your left foot?*

- Hypothesising: *What might happen if you…?*

- Problem solving: *How can you speed up input times without making mistakes?*

- Evaluation: *How effective is your organisation's health and safety policy?*

Again, this is where taxonomies of learning can help you set more challenging questions in a planned way, by deliberately moving the learner up to the next level of the taxonomy. It also helps the learner with their skills of critical reflection because you are asking them to look critically at their own knowledge and performance.

Key term

Critical reflection: A way of reviewing personal progress and development

Activity: Planning one-to-one coaching

Here's a framework to use when running a one-to-one coaching session. It is similar to a session plan but with much more interaction between you and your learner. To see whether it works for you, think of one of your learners who may need coaching in your vocational area and make notes on what needs to happen at each stage.

Stage	What I need to do	What my learner needs to do
1 **Create the right climate for learning to take place**	Make sure there are no distractions	
2 **Share learning objectives**	Refer back to the learner's individual learning plan (ILP) where appropriate	
3 **Recap on the previous session**	Possibly model the performance if the learner has forgotten	
4 **Ask questions to check understanding**	Give feedback on the answers	
5 **Ask the learner to perform a task**	Observe	
6 **Ask the learner what worked**	Listen	
7 **Ask the learner what didn't work**	Listen	
8 **Give feedback**	Comment on what you saw them do (or not do) and whether or not it worked in your opinion	
9 **Ask the learner to repeat the task, incorporating your feedback and theirs**	Ask the learner to talk you through what they are doing this time and give them feedback	
10 **Repeat steps 3–8 as necessary**	Refine the learner's performance until you are both confident that they have achieved the learning objectives	
11 **Agree learning objectives for the next session**	Document them so that you can use them for planning your next session	

Developing learners' expertise

Coaching techniques are particularly useful once learners have acquired the basics and are starting to develop expertise in their job. One indicator of this is when they can be allowed to get on with the job or task in hand with little or no supervision.

When coaching learners to develop their expertise, it is a good idea to do the following:

- **Encourage deeper knowledge.** This is about asking your learner open-ended questions to make their learning visible to them, and to challenge them. Think in terms of having a learning conversation, where you both ask open-ended questions beginning with 'What', 'Why', 'When', 'Where' and 'How', and find answers or solutions together.

- **Negotiate learning objectives with learners.** Encourage them to take ownership of their learning. For example, if you encounter a work problem that neither of you has come across before, find out how others in the company have resolved it and set an objective for your learner to find out more.

- **Ask your learner to reflect on how well they are doing.** Learners need the ability to be self-critical if they are to improve performance. Experts internalise this process and are self-critical as a matter of routine. (See Chapter 5 for ways of encouraging learners to reflect.)

- **See problems as a source of learning.** This means deliberately exposing learners to problems that are increasingly complex. Experts come up against complex problems every day in their jobs. Finding ways to tackle increasingly complex problems successfully is a good way to improve practice. Examples might be a joiner working with a new type of wood for the first time or a carer dealing with an elderly patient with a medical condition they haven't come across before.

- **Make sure that learners' English, mathematics and ICT are satisfactory.** Don't just map these skills across to qualifications or teach them in isolation; instead, make them relevant to the work activities the learner does and teach them so that they can see how they contribute to getting better at the tasks they do. (For more on embedding English, mathematics and ICT teaching, see pages 51–9.)

The 'inner game'

As a tennis coach, Timothy Gallwey (1974)[12] first noticed that his coachees' performance improved faster when he adopted a questioning approach rather than telling them what to do. He found that they identified for themselves the small adjustments to performance they needed to make and that, by internalising these, they were able to relax and focus more. His 'inner game' methods have since been widely adopted in coaching.

The GROW model of coaching

The GROW model of the coaching process is based on setting specific goals aimed at changing behaviour and solving problems and is one of the models most relevant to work-based learning. You will find it useful to follow if you work regularly with learners on an individual basis and are responsible for improving their technical skills.

GROW stands for:

Goal: This step corresponds to your learning objectives and is where you define and agree with your learner what they will achieve.

Reality: You then define where the learner is now, which might involve carrying out (self-)assessment and giving feedback.

Obstacles/Options: Next, you identify the obstacles in the way of the learner achieving the goals and look for ways of overcoming them. This means specifying any barriers in the way of learning and choosing ways of meeting their goals that are best suited to the coaching situation.

Way forward: Once you've chosen the options, you agree a plan of action for the learner to achieve their goals.

---

12 W. Timothy Gallwey (1974), *The Inner Game of Tennis* (1st edn). New York: Random House.

Demonstration, instruction and presentation

These three strategies come under the 'trainer-led' heading. This is because it's you, the trainer, doing most of the action or talking. Demonstrations are for showing learners how something is done when you are introducing them to new tasks and skills. Instruction is used for taking learners through a task or principle step by step. A presentation is a good way of explaining knowledge – concepts or new ideas – to groups of learners.

The opposite of a presentation is to ask the learner to find something out for themselves. This is sometimes called discovery learning, investigative learning, research-based learning or 'flipped' learning. It can be a useful way of encouraging learners' research skills and can be individuals working on their own or in small groups. Learners then share what they have learned with one another and with you.

'Some of our learners have a low reading age and a very short concentration span. You have to say it once slowly and make sure you use words they understand. Then you have to say it again – and again, until they say "Oh, so what you mean is…" and repeat it back to you. Otherwise there's no way they've understood.'
Trainer

Key terms

Surface knowledge: Recalling facts and figures without always demonstrating understanding

Deep learning: Making connections between ideas, concepts and previous experiences and applying that learning to different situations; in other words, the learning has become part of the individual and their performance. You are aiming for deep learning when developing learners' expertise.

Flipped learning: Where work normally carried out during a session is 'flipped' to outside the session

Demonstration

The purpose of a demonstration is to show learners the 'whole' picture – a procedure, process or task – in a relatively short time. You would normally follow a demonstration with instruction if you wanted learners to be able to do the task or follow the procedure themselves.

Think carefully about whether a demonstration is the best method to use in a given situation. For example, an online video might serve the purpose better. You might know of someone who's more experienced than you who might be available to deliver the demonstration you have in mind. You also need to think about whether you can keep it short enough to retain the interest of your learners. If it is any longer than 20 minutes, learners will lose concentration. They also need to be able to follow the demonstration with a related activity or task if you have set an objective concerning their ability to practise or do the task itself.

A video will also enable you to observe the learners while they are watching the video, which will allow you to gauge their level of interest and commitment to what is being demonstrated. If you are demonstrating yourself, you will be busy and engaged on the demonstration and probably not notice what is happening for your learners.

Activity: Preparing a demonstration

Here's a question-and-answer checklist to use when choosing a demonstration and preparing it.

	Question	Yes	No
1	Do learners need to see the task or process?	☐	☐
2	Am I confident that this is the most efficient way to show them?	☐	☐
3	Is this the most suitable delivery method for this situation?	☐	☐
4	Can I fit the demonstration into about 20 minutes?	☐	☐
5	Do I have all the equipment I need?	☐	☐
6	Have I planned for learners' questions at key stages and/or at the end?	☐	☐
7	Can everyone see and hear?	☐	☐
8	Have I planned for learners to follow up the demonstration, and perhaps take notes?	☐	☐

You are aiming for a yes in each case. If you answered no to questions 1 to 3, you might ask yourself whether a demonstration is the best approach. If you answered no to questions 4 to 8, you will need to address the problem.

Instruction

Instruction is a good method to use when learners are completely new to a task or procedure, or need to be taken through a task until they get it right. It's where you explain and tell them what to do, step by step. However, it's not a good strategy to use once learners are competent, because it does not encourage them to think or do things for themselves. Once you are confident that learners understand the task and can do it (albeit in an unskilled way), you will need to adopt a more hands-off method – such as individual coaching – for performance to improve.

Here are some ways of involving learners when using instruction:

- **Instruct them in a 'straight line'.** This is where you start at the beginning and take the learner through a task to the end (think of a cookery demonstration where the ingredients have to be added in a certain order). You can ask individual learners to take over at any point, and ask others to help if they fall behind or don't know what to do next.

- **Start in the middle.** You can use this instructional technique during a second session, when you're recapping or checking what the learner has remembered. You can ask, 'What do you do to get this far?' or 'What happens next?', and ask the learner to show you.

- **Trainer and learner take turns.** This is a useful technique to use when practising skills, processes or procedures. Ask learners to take a turn and talk you – and the rest of the group if you have more than one learner – through what they are doing, and why.

- **Start at the end and work backwards, or dismantle a piece of equipment.** Use this technique when you want to see what learners can remember, and where things go.

'When we're laying bricks in the workshop, there's always one or two who get it straight off. You can start them off then leave them to get on. Then there are the ones who need a bit of help. I use the "take turns" method. I do a line of bricks to start with, then I get them to take the trowel and do a bit or take turns with each other. There are always some who can't measure straight, so you have to concentrate on that aspect of the task until they get it right. I do it all ways – like breaking tasks into much smaller stages and showing them exactly what I want them to do and pairing them up with the better ones. It's a tricky time as the trainer, starting them off. You have to spend as long as it takes because they can't progress until they can lay bricks in a straight line.'
Trainer

'I use the EDIP mnemonic (Explain, Demonstrate, Imitate, Practice) when I'm skills training: I do the first two, then it's over to the learner for the next two.'
Trainer

Presentation

A presentation is good for explaining knowledge to a large group of learners. However, presentations don't by themselves demand anything from the learner other than the ability to watch, listen and recall key points or facts. You need to follow up a presentation with another method or methods. In addition, the success of a presentation usually depends on your skills as a presenter and your ability to get the information across in an interesting and engaging way.

Good reasons to use a presentation include:

- when you want to explain or interpret facts and figures

- when you want to put forward an argument or point of view

- when you want to change how people think or behave (think 'motivational speaker').

Remember

Instruction isn't just a case of showing or telling learners something once, or even twice. You may need to use a variety of techniques to achieve your learning objectives and maintain their interest until you are confident that they can do the task. You may also have to repeat things regularly.

Presentation top tips

Here's a list of top tips given to one trainer by her group of 16-year-olds after she had given a presentation:

- Slow down.

- Keep it short.

- Use short words that we understand.

- Don't use too many slides.

- Don't play with Blu-Tack.

- Don't use red or green (some of us can't read it!).

- Ask more questions.

- Give us the notes afterwards.

Activity: *Preparing a presentation*

The following checklist will help you decide whether or not a presentation is appropriate.

Question		Yes	No
1	Do a large number of learners need to know this?	☐	☐
2	Do they all need to know it at the same time?	☐	☐
3	Can I structure my presentation into stages, and sum it up using three or four key points?	☐	☐
4	Have I considered whether a handout, a discussion or an assignment would work just as well?	☐	☐
5	Am I good at putting across concepts and explaining them?	☐	☐
6	Will it take no more than 20 minutes' talking on my part?	☐	☐
7	Have I considered ways of involving my learners, and can I prove it?	☐	☐
8	Have I ever recorded myself delivering a presentation and watched it?	☐	☐

You should be able to answer yes to every question before you use a presentation.

Involving learners

By definition, a presentation can only convey something to the learner. If you want them to be able to know or do something, or behave differently as a result of your input, you will need to follow up a presentation with more active methods for the learner during your session. The following table gives suggestions for these.

Area of learning	Follow up with ...
Knowing (cognitive): To help learners assimilate what you've said	Oral questioning Handouts with notes
...or to test what they've remembered	Multiple-choice questions A verbal or written test
How to behave (affective): To identify changes in behaviour or attitude	Topics for discussion groups Questions or issues for pair work

Group work

Group work is usually an active process for learners, because it is they, not the trainer, who are doing the talking or carrying out a task. The job of the trainer here is usually to facilitate the work by introducing the task, keeping the group(s) on time and on task, offering help and clarification, and then overseeing the debrief, where small groups feed back to the whole group.

Working in small groups allows learners to collaborate, discuss and try out the methods, principles, ideas or processes they are learning about. Importantly, quieter learners will often actively contribute to a small group when they might not to a larger one. Small groups take advantage of the interests, experience and expertise of other group members. Well-managed group work not only increases attention to task but also helps develop subject-specific communication and teamworking skills.

When planning group work, you will need to take into account:

- the different abilities of your learners
- how you will split your learners into small groups
- how you will brief your learners (What do you want them to do?)
- the time you will have available
- any resources you will need, including enough space to carry out your planned activities.

When to use group work

Here are some of the areas where learning in small groups works best:

- Learning in the affective domain (values, attitudes and how people behave)
- Collaborative tasks that require members of the small group to combine their expertise and work together, or where the task you have set has multiple components
- Process skills training (for example, teamwork)
- Discussing issues: topics where there is no right answer or you need to reach a consensus
- Generating ideas.

> **Remember**
>
> A small group usually means three to six learners; any more and people are less likely to join in.

Formats for group work

This table shows the various formats you can choose from for group work.

Same task, different tasks	Groups can work on the same task or different ones at the same time. You can introduce an element of competition or a reward to motivate people, if appropriate.
Snowballs	Pairs join with other pairs to make a four; fours join to make an eight. This is useful for introductions and for comparing and sharing information, or if you have a large or lively group that likes to talk.
Pairs and peer work	This is useful in mixed-ability groups where you can pair up experienced with inexperienced learners. Pairs are also good for debating, where you deliberately get each person to argue for or against a particular strategy or idea.
Triads	Here, learners work in threes. Triads are good for role plays in pairs where you need a third person to observe and feed back.
Buzz groups	Here, you allocate small groups a series of topics and get them to discuss each topic for about five minutes before moving on to the next topic.
Syndicates and plenary	These are often used at conferences, where members of a large group select or are allocated a smaller group to take on a particular task or subject, and which then reports back to the main group.

Limitations of group work

Here are some of the things to watch out for:

- Learners can get bored if groups are badly managed or used as a substitute for training.

- There's a danger of 'passengers' – learners who don't contribute to the group task.

- Success often relies on contributions from individual members – such as the ability to observe and feed back – but you can't always rely on inexperienced learners to have these skills.

- You need plenty of workshop space if you are planning practical activities and good seating arrangements (around tables, work benches or computers) for group activities involving talking, thinking and writing.

Debriefing group work

You need to leave enough time at the end of the group work to summarise with your learners what they have done. Your skill as a trainer here is in how you summarise the work of the groups and bring them back together into one group. Having a prepared list of aims and learning objectives for the session to refer to is useful at this point, as you can look at these and gauge whether or not they have been met. You can do this by involving the whole group.

Here are some debriefing tips:

- If all groups have completed the same task, ask for one key point from each group (so that the last group has something to share); you can continue with a second round of key points if necessary.

- Always leave enough time to take feedback from your learners as a result of group work, particularly if you've set the groups a discussion task or asked them to come up with ideas.

- Try to capture the main points on a flipchart, smartboard or similar. You can ask a member of each small group to do this, getting each of them to present back in turn. Be aware, though, if you have appointed someone to capture the main points, that not everyone is a skilled listener or writer. Also, allow time in your session planning for small groups to report back to the whole group, and then to discuss their responses.

- If you do the writing on a flipchart, smartboard or similar as you receive the feedback, you will need to turn your back to the group and think on your feet as you write. Check that you capture the main points with the small group as you write up what they are saying.

- Check your spelling and punctuation. If you make an error, your learners might think it is the correct form, as they expect you to know everything!

Projects and assignments

You will have many opportunities to use projects and assignments in your vocational area or programme, but it is important to be aware of when they are the most appropriate method of delivering learning. For example, in the workplace, projects and assignments are a good way of involving employers in identifying a relevant topic for the learner. Similarly, if you are the employer, you can ask the training providers you work with to show you projects that are relevant to you, or devise your own.

Projects and assignments can be either classroom-based, involving research, or purely practical, or a mixture. Have a look at the following project examples: the first is classroom-based, and the second is a practical project. What does the learner need to know and be able to do to complete each one successfully? Compare your thoughts with those below and add any further knowledge or skills you think are relevant.

Key terms

Project: An investigation or exercise involving practical activities and tasks

Assignment: Usually a problem-solving activity with a clear brief, a structured framework, guidelines on how to carry it out, a specified length (often in the form of a word count) and a time limit

Project 1

Plan a day's outing for a group of children from your nursery by researching attractions and places to visit in your local area. Produce a budget and an itinerary.

Learners will need to know...

- the local area
- how to find information
- appropriate activities for children
- the legal aspects, such as safeguarding and health and safety
- the transport options.

Learners need to be able to...

- plan their work
- calculate timings and costs
- produce a budget
- draw up an itinerary.

Project 2

Plan for an evening's service at a restaurant

Learners will need to know...

- how to set a table according to company guidelines, including:
  - folding napkins
  - setting out cutlery and tableware
- the content of the evening menu
- staffing levels.

Learners need to be able to...

- set out tables according to bookings
- lay tables appropriately, according to company guidelines
- liaise with the chef
- allocate tables to waiting staff
- liaise with kitchen staff as appropriate.

It can be tempting to give learners a project or assignment before they are ready, because it requires learners to do most of the work. However, you can see from the above examples that the trainer would need to do quite a lot of training and preparation before learners could carry out either project successfully, and even then they would still need the trainer's help and support.

Activity: Structuring a research assignment

Research assignments are where you want learners to find things out for themselves. Here's a way to structure one over a number of sessions or visits to learners. Read through what happens at each stage. Then think of a possible topic for your own learner or learners, and write down ideas for activities you might include at each stage.

Stage	What happens	Ideas for activities
1 **Engage learners**	You introduce the topic and your learning objectives with a group of learners; or you negotiate relevant learning objectives with an individual. You and your learners discuss the topic. You help connect the topic with learners' prior knowledge and experience (so they can see the benefits of doing it).	
2 **Build inquiry and research skills**	Learners identify information that will help them and ways of getting it. Learners develop a project plan. You help learners design research tools such as questionnaires or interviews.	
3 **Learners investigate**	Learners research the topic and collect information using a variety of methods (the Internet, books, carrying out surveys or interviews, etc.).	
4 **Learners analyse what they've found**	Learners organise their findings (this could mean producing graphs, pie charts or grouping their data). You help them check the reliability of their sources (particularly if they've been using the Internet). Learners analyse their findings and discuss what they mean.	
5 **Learners synthesise, summarise and draw conclusions**	Learners re-examine their findings, summarise their ideas and draw conclusions.	

Stage	What happens	Ideas for activities
6 **Learners produce something as a result of their findings and conclusions**	Learners decide on the best way of communicating their findings: If their findings are mainly knowledge or attitude-based, they could produce a report or a slide presentation. If it's a practical project, they might produce a product – a model, machine, photographs, or a combination of these.	
7 **Learners reflect on and evaluate their own work**	Learners present the results of their projects and defend their findings (which means they need to understand them).	
8 **Learners do extension work**	You design extension activities that will help learners apply what they've learned to new situations and experiences. Alternatively, you ask learners themselves how they would like to extend their project or what they would like to do next.	

A project for an employer

Here is an example of a practical project based on an employer's needs. In this example, the employer needed to redesign part of the warehouse where different timbers were stored. The employer asked the learner to do this and then present their findings and recommendations. Here is the approach to the project that the learner and trainer agreed:

Stage	Tasks to carry out	Things to remember
1 **Draw up a project plan**	Identify the materials to be stored and the risks. Research the storage options available using suppliers' online catalogues. Choose storage solutions and justify your choice.	Specify conditions needed for materials to remain in good condition. Ask about timescales and delivery. Consider in-house options.
2 **Produce costings**	Include costs for: • shelving/storage • other refurbishment costs (replacement doors and windows, paint).	List equipment that must be replaced. Include discounts if available. Show alternatives.
3 **Create a scale diagram of the storage area**	Measure up the area. Produce a scale diagram. Design the storage area, indicating where each product is to be stored.	Include health and safety factors: fire hazards; fire extinguishers; safety signs. Allow enough room for access.
4 **Make recommendations**	Present the scale diagram and costings to management.	Be prepared to incorporate changes to plans as necessary.

The project plans were approved and the learner was then asked to plan and oversee the ordering and erection of new shelving and storage.

Games, icebreakers, role plays and simulations

Games, icebreakers, role-plays and simulations are potentially enjoyable ways of delivering learning, when used in the right context. Icebreakers are usually used at the beginning of a course to enable everyone to get to know one another.

Games

Games can be a light-hearted way of getting across a serious point. They are also good for increasing energy levels or breaking the ice at the beginning of a course, and for stimulating discussion. They are also an essential way of learning and demonstrating 'soft' skills such as communicating with others and establishing particular attitudes and behaviours.

You can introduce an element of competition or fun into most learning topics by turning them into games or challenges. In the workplace, you can use games to introduce an element of competition between learners. Here too, you might use a game or competition to increase speed or accuracy if learners are at the stage of needing to practise a skill in order to improve performance. You don't have to complicate things: it might just be a case of introducing teams and scores, a board and dice or timed activities.

Here are some games you could adapt to fit your vocational area.

The 'What would you do if...?' game

This game gets learners to examine their attitudes to their work and helps them reflect on how they would respond in a given situation, and compare their own responses to those of their co-learners. You prepare for the game by writing scenarios linked to your learners' jobs or the topic and ask teams to score one another's responses. Here are some examples from the care sector:

What would you do if...

- a resident wandered into another's room while he was getting dressed?

- a relative accused you of stealing from her mother's purse?

- staff ignore the weekly fire alarm and carry on working?

'I use this game during induction. Learners are usually very fixed about what they'd do or put up with before they start the job. When they've been out on placement for a few weeks we play it again and I remind them of their original responses. By this time, many of them have had to deal with the scenarios for real. One learner said she'd leave if she had to deal with an aggressive client, whereas in practice she was very calm.'

Trainer, care sector

Pass the parcel

This game is good for discussing case studies. Here, the trainer breaks down a whole case study into a sequence of events and writes each event on a different piece of paper. Examples could be a series of faults within vehicle maintenance, a customer's case file, or a situation (such as fitting gas pipes) that escalates into an emergency. Each event is then wrapped into a different layer of a parcel (with a small prize wrapped inside the first layer if appropriate). Learners pass the parcel to music, unwrapping one layer at a time and taking turns to read out each event and saying what they would do. The rest of the group then responds and adds ideas.

Remember

If your learners expect to be taken seriously, they may react negatively to playing games and feel patronised, so it's a good idea to explain the point of a game to them beforehand. To be effective, just say something like, 'Everyone's nodding off. Let's do a quick round of—.' You can also avoid a negative reaction by calling it an activity rather than a game.

Key term

Induction: The process of learners getting to know one another and the trainer giving information about the programme

'As part of our employability programme, we expect all learners to find their own work experience. We get them to take turns at pitching in front of a panel of local employers who then give them feedback and offer them a placement if they come across well. When preparing them, we treat it like a game, but they take it very seriously indeed, as do the employers.'
Employability trainer

'My colleagues and I make good use of matching card games. I train assessors and I have two sets of cards, one with learning objectives and another with the assessment methods. I give them out to the trainee assessors and ask them to find their pair. It gets them moving as well as thinking.'
Teacher trainer

Remember

Be aware of the cultural context when choosing games and rewards: for example, in some cultures anything related to gambling is frowned upon.

Icebreakers

Icebreakers are activities designed to help people get to know one another at the beginning of a programme of learning. Always make sure they are suitable and appropriate for your group of learners. Here are some examples.

Meet your partner

This is a variation of asking each learner to introduce themselves to the group, which can be a bit intimidating if they don't know anyone else. Put the learners into pairs and ask everyone to talk to their partner for five minutes about their interests, their reason for attending and their expectations. They may find they have something in common and create a bond. You then ask each person to introduce the person they have been talking to to the group.

A good idea is to note down your learners' names when they introduce each other, on a rough sketch of a seating plan. This will help you remember their names – it's likely that they will return to the same position at the next session. Making a note of their expectations will help you match what they expect with what the programme involves. If the programme will not be covering one or more of their expectations, make sure you explain why this is.

Speed dating

This is a good icebreaker to use if your learners don't know anyone else, because everyone gets the chance to introduce themselves to several other people. Here, you ask learners to sit on two lines of chairs facing each other and give pairs a minute or two to share information about themselves, their jobs and/or their reasons for learning, before moving on to the next person.

Cats, horses and dogs

This is good to use at the beginning of a programme with groups of mixed levels of knowledge or abilities. It gives everyone permission to be themselves and allows you to identify any experts whose knowledge and skills you can draw on, and any who lack confidence. Give the descriptions of each animal and ask participants to say which one they identify with the most.

Cats: their own bosses, choosing where they go and what they do. These are usually the confident ones who may already know/can do a lot.

Horses: fast, hard-working and reliable. People who identify themselves as horses are usually those with some knowledge and skills and who are attending to learn more or to improve their skills.

Dogs: intelligent, willing to learn anything new, enthusiastic. People who identify themselves as dogs are usually those new to your area of training.

Stress that everyone is allowed to ask any questions they like.

Bingo

This is an active icebreaker that requires everyone to stand up, move around and chat to other people. Learners need a pen or a pencil and the following handout (which you could adapt and make smaller or bigger, depending on your group). When you say 'Go', learners ask a question from the sheet to one other person and then write their name down in the question's box. They then move on to someone else, but can go back to the same person later if there are not many in the group. Only one question can be asked to one person at a time. You can decide whether they need to fill a line, a diagonal or a column, or indeed the full grid. The learner who achieves this first shouts 'Bingo!'

Key point

If you don't have time for introductions, you could issue name badges for learners to wear or name cards to place in front of them. This acts as a visual reminder to others, and helps you remember and use their name when speaking to them.

Speaks a foreign language	Owns a cat	Has a job	Has been to Europe	Has a mobile device with them
Has blue eyes	Has been to Asia or India	Rides a motorbike	Is a vegetarian or vegan	Lives within six miles of here
Lives more than six miles from here	Has been outside Europe	Owns a dog	Enjoys gardening	Likes swimming
Has children or stepchildren	Has come here by car	Has brown eyes	Is nervous about taking this course	Has green eyes
Has a bicycle	Is going on holiday soon	Has a spare pen and paper	Has come here by train or bus	Has been to the USA or Canada

Icebreakers can also be used during a particular session, perhaps at the beginning (as a 'starter activity') or after a break to help learners refocus (as an 'energiser'). As your learners will already know each other, you can devise activities such as a quiz or a game based on the current topic, or something active that gets learners moving about and is appropriate to the age range and maturity of your learners.

Setting ground rules

Ground rules are boundaries and rules to help create suitable conditions within which learners (and you) can safely work and learn. They should underpin appropriate behaviour and respect for everyone in the group, including you, and allow the session to run smoothly. If they are not set, problems may occur that could disrupt the session and lead to misunderstandings or behaviour problems. It is best to agree ground rules during the first meeting, perhaps after the icebreaker once everyone is feeling more relaxed.

Ground rules should always be discussed and negotiated with your learners rather than forced on them. You can agree ground rules with individual learners as well as groups. Using an activity to do this will help learners feel included, so that they will be more likely to take ownership of the rules and follow them. Some ground rules might be renegotiated or added to throughout the programme; for example, changing the break time or how personal devices will be used. Others might be non-negotiable: for example, health and safety requirements. The types of ground rules you agree with your learners will depend on their age and maturity.

Role plays

Role plays make useful 'dry runs' for challenges your learners will face in the real workplace. They are a good way of practising skills under controlled conditions: you can get learners to run through situations safely and within the boundaries you set. They are good for:

- practising 'people' or communication skills

- practising interview techniques

- getting learners to see themselves as others see them

- experiencing and dealing with feelings in a controlled way

- dealing with awkward situations (for example, difficult callers or customers)

- asking learners to put themselves in another's position and/or to deliberately act in a certain way (and see what happens…as long as it's safe to do so)

- asking learners to take turns in a different role (such as trainer, learner and observer; or customer and member of staff).

You need to be careful about what you ask learners to do during role plays, and not set them up to look foolish in front of others. You may also need to manage learners' expectations. Some learners don't like 'play acting' so you would need to tell them the objectives of the exercise and how they will benefit. Consider, too, that the extent to which learners learn will depend on the limits of their acting abilities. You cannot expect them to demonstrate the skills you want them to learn if others are unable to act out their part in the role play!

'I employed a professional actor to help with our customer service training. He was so convincing that it was just like the real thing. None of the learners thought, "This is stupid." Instead, they were truly challenged and ended up briefing the actor to run through some of their most difficult situations with them.'
Trainer, customer service

'If the objective is around the affective rather than psychomotor domain, a safer alternative to role play is a version of sculpting. Key roles in a scenario are written on pieces of paper. These are put on the floor and learners stand on one, "in the role". They do not act out the scenario, but think themselves into the role and then tell the group how they feel and what they might do in that situation. They can talk with other characters or other learners and the trainer can ask them questions. It is still experiential and can help develop or challenge attitudes, but does not require any acting skills.'
Teacher trainer

'It is really important to debrief any role play so that learners can come out of the role and leave any feelings behind in the training room. I experienced this myself as part of social work training: the role play itself was excellent but the debrief was poor and I went home shaking and feeling sick.'
Teacher trainer

Activity: Planning a role play

Role plays need to be carefully planned and set up. Use the following checklist to help you plan your role play. You are aiming to answer yes in each case.

Question	Yes	No
1 Have you ensured that your learners have the skills to act out the situations required for the role play to be successful?	☐	☐
2 Have you set learning objectives for the role play that your learners will relate to and be able to achieve?	☐	☐
3 Have you planned who does what and written any guidelines needed?	☐	☐
4 Have you told your learners the point of the role play?	☐	☐
5 Have you briefed your learners and set timings for each part of the role play?	☐	☐
6 Have you planned what you want to get out of the debrief, set some time aside for it and thought about how you will do it?	☐	☐

Simulations

In a simulation you create an environment that's as close to the real thing as possible and use this for teaching and learning purposes. This is sometimes known as a realistic working environment (RWE): think of restaurants, hairdressing and beauty salons in a college, a construction site where learners build for 'real', or using facsimiles of parts of the body when starting to teach clinical procedures. Simulations are also good for situations where safety, cost or confidentiality mean that you can't teach in a real-life setting. For example, you might use a simulation for:

- training in the use of expensive or potentially dangerous equipment

- health and safety procedures

- first aid

- dealing with accidents or major incidents

- fault-finding and fixing.

As with a role play, a simulation needs careful planning and preparation. You need to have clear learning objectives in mind at the outset, and carry out a structured debrief afterwards. Be aware, however, that some qualifications specifically exclude simulations as part of the assessment methodology. While simulations are a good learning method in many cases, don't assume that you can use them for assessment.

Activity: Reflecting on delivery methods

It's easy to adopt the methods you feel most comfortable with and keep using them until they become the norm. An interesting and useful exercise is to reflect on how true this is of you. Part 1 of the activity below asks you to reflect on the methods you currently use. Part 2 asks you to try out a method you haven't used before and reflect on how well it went.

Part 1: Reflecting on your delivery methods

Answer the following questions as honestly as you can, and reflect on how you might try out new or different approaches with your learners.

Question	Answer
1 What methods do you use most, and why?	
2 What do your learners think about them? (Ask them about the approaches *they* prefer.)	
3 Are their answers different from yours? What does this tell you?	
4 Could you use other methods? If so, list which ones and how you might introduce them. (Refer to the table listing the different delivery strategies on page 74.)	

Part 2: Trying a new delivery method

Try introducing one of the methods that you've identified in answer to question 4 above. When you have done so, reflect on how it went by answering the following questions:

Question	Answer
1 What were learners' reactions?	
2 How did the delivery method you chose contribute to their learning (if at all)?	

3 How did you feel about using this method?	
4 What does this tell you?	
5 How successful was the method?	
6 Would you use this method again? If so, how and why? If not, why not?	

Choosing and using resources

An important part of planning any training session is to choose resources that will support the delivery methods you use and therefore enable learners to achieve the learning objectives you have set. For workplace learners this will mean making use of resources from their real working environment as far as possible.

Another main factor influencing your choice of resources will depend on in which of the domains you have set your learning objectives. For example:

Domain	Consider the following resources
Knowledge (cognitive)	Handouts; slides and a laptop/mobile device; access to computers and the Internet; books
Doing (psychomotor)	The real thing: such as the actual tools and equipment for the tasks you've set as your learning objectives (for example, 'to bake a Victoria sponge' would mean having the ingredients, cooking equipment and a kitchen)
Attitude (affective)	Projects; visits; 'real-life' experiences such as work shadowing; games, role plays and case studies; 'real' people – speakers who can answer learners' questions.

'We invested in e-learning modules and a virtual learning environment where tutors and learners could talk to one another and share assignments and resources. Unfortunately, we didn't take account of our learners: most of them lack the digital skills you need to get going. Nobody used the forums we set up. Our tutors were just the same – they are all highly skilled trainers, but were reluctant to run online tutorials when they were used to seeing learners face to face. We'd completely overlooked this!'

Training manager

Other factors to consider when choosing resources are:

- **Cost.** This includes the time involved in producing them, and ensuring that you don't reinvent what has been done before.

- **Group size versus one to one.** You'll be looking at economies of scale if you are teaching groups of learners. For example, showing an online video to a group is cheaper than taking them on a visit. Similarly, if you only deal with learners on a one-to-one basis, consider using resources that will broaden their experience.

- **The environment.** You must ensure that learners are working in a safe environment, with enough space and the right equipment to carry out the activities and use the resources you have planned. Health and safety considerations are important if you are teaching practical skills involving potentially hazardous tools, equipment or substances – for example teaching learners welding skills or how to use power tools. In addition, if learners come into contact with heat, electrical, chemical or biohazards, your resources must include personal protective equipment (PPE) to guard them against potential infection or injury. If you are using resources in the working environment, you may need to visit premises in advance and/or assess any risks involved to ensure their safety.

- **Accessibility and availability.** Can you access the resources? Can all your learners use them easily?

- **Your ability to use them effectively.** If you lack confidence in designing resources such as a handout, or you can't express yourself clearly, or you're not familiar enough with digital technologies for e-learning, you will need to update your skills.

'We were thinking of producing our own in-house resources for health and social care when I discovered online modules. You pay a subscription per learner to access them and it worked out a lot cheaper.'
Trainer

> ## Remember
>
> Inclusive practice is about ensuring that all learners have equal access to learning according to their needs: it doesn't mean training them all in exactly the same way. For example, producing a written handout might not be suitable for learners with low literacy levels. Similarly, using e-modules may assume that all learners have access to high-speed broadband and the Internet. You also need to consider learners with physical or mobility problems if you are planning activities requiring dexterity or a full range of movement.

Activity: Choosing appropriate resources

Use the following checklist when choosing teaching and learning resources.

Question	Yes	No
1 Is this resource easily available and accessible to my learners? (Can they all see it, hear it and/or use it?)	☐	☐
2 Is it appropriate to the topic and learning domain? (For example, using desk-based e-learning for learning objectives in the psychomotor domain would be inappropriate.)	☐	☐
3 Have I addressed any health and safety issues associated with the resources or equipment I plan to use?	☐	☐
4 Is it cost-effective? (Do you know it's the cheapest or most efficient alternative because you've researched what's available?)	☐	☐
5 Is it suitable for the size of the group?	☐	☐
6 Is it suitable for the learning environment?	☐	☐
7 Am I comfortable about using this resource/equipment?	☐	☐

You are aiming to answer yes in each case. Where you've answered no, you may need to rethink your choice of resources. If you answered no to the last question, you will need to plan some training or practice in using the resource.

Here are some tips on designing and using some of the most common training and learning resources.

Screens, slides and visuals

A good slide or visual:

- summarises your key points

- fits into the whole, with one slide following on logically from the previous one as part of the narrative

- supports what you have to say (as opposed to you reading each slide out loud)

- has a consistent design

- uses text sparingly (try the 6 x 6 rule: a maximum of six key points with a maximum of six words per point)

- has no spelling mistakes or bad grammar

- is written in upper and lower case, not all in capital letters

- isn't too busy or distracting, with appropriate use of animation, transitions, colours, etc.

- makes good use of colour: for example, use of a 'spot' colour to highlight headings and bullet points (but remember to watch your use of red and green in case learners have difficulty discerning these colours)

- contains only carefully selected visuals that convey meaning or make a point.

A good presenter:

- uses the tried-and-tested format – 'Tell them what you're going to tell them, then tell them, then tell them what you've told them' – to structure their presentation

- prepares detailed notes and practises what they are going to say first, preferably in front of a critical audience, such as colleagues

- produces a list of prompts to remind them of their key points rather than reading from notes

- talks about the slide (they already know what they are going to say and what comes next – they don't read off the slide word for word, but face the audience and not the screen)

- doesn' t walk or stand in front of the screen, blocking parts of it from view

- allows time for learners to assimilate what they've said: by talking clearly, pausing, and allowing learners to read or make notes.

'I use flipchart a lot in my training. When I'm using prepared flipcharts, I write the last activity first. In this way, when I turn to the flipchart, I have the sheets in order and don't have to go through pages to get to the one I want. I also use post-it notes on the corner of the page so I can turn to pages I want quickly without fumbling. I add notes to my session plan saying "room/resource prep", so I know what I have to do before the session starts. Of course, if the group changes so will the session; even the same subject is different with different groups.'
Teacher trainer

Digital learning tools and new technologies

Many of the tools you can use to support training and learning come under the broad heading of digital or new technologies. This section will enable you to:

- identify some of the tools and when to use them

- make decisions about how technology can support what you are trying to achieve, and therefore when to include them as part of your overall training and learning strategy and/or when to use them with learners.

Key point

This section is not a comprehensive guide to digital learning and you should be prepared to do further research of your own. Computer specialists rather than trainers often choose the hardware and software, but don't be afraid to reject a particular package if it doesn't support learning objectives or learners' needs. Mass-produced e-learning packages can sometimes be repetitive or poorly designed, so always check that they meet the needs of your learners before you buy.

The use of digital tools should form part of your teaching and learning strategy if you think they will support your overall aims and learning objectives. The following research into e-portfolios puts it like this:

'[Tools such as] e-portfolio systems … form part of a strategic approach to learning and teaching – it is the pedagogy, not the tool, that comes first.'
Effective Practice with e-Portfolios, JISC (2008)[13]

Further considerations for trainers include learner expectations, the pace of technological change and your own ability to keep up with developments and how they apply to your vocational area.

Don't make the mistake of assuming your learners know more about digital technology than you do. The following statement sums up research findings into learners' expectations of digital technology. It underlines the trainer's responsibility for making the right choices concerning its suitability and for providing a supportive learning environment:

'The so-called Google generation has high expectations of digital technology, for example that it will be robust, flexible, responsive to their individual needs and available anywhere. However, many learners do not have a clear understanding of how courses could or should use technology to support learning. They are still reliant on lecturers [trainers] for guidance … While many practitioners feel that their "digitally native" learners are running ahead of them, there is evidence that age is not the main determining factor in technology confidence and capability: a supportive context, for example, is far more significant … practitioners [trainers] therefore have a critical role to play.'
Responding to Learners, Guide 2, JISC (2009)[14]

Blended learning

Blended learning is where a range of learning methods is used in a programme, and it increasingly means a mixture of face-to-face and digital methods. The following are all examples of such blended learning approaches. The third bullet is an example of 'flipped' learning:

- Face-to-face training sessions followed by individual coaching face to face or online (using Skype or similar)

- Small-group training via classroom seminars, or increasingly by webinars followed by assignments and individual online tutorials (either visually, aurally or by written text)

- Online and text-based research prior to a training session, which is then discussed when the group comes together

- Use of an online virtual learning environment (VLE) for peer discussions and individual feedback from you, the trainer, on work they have uploaded.

---

13 http://webarchive.nationalarchives.gov.uk/20140702233839/http:/www.jisc.ac.uk/media/documents/publications/effectivepracticeeportfolios.pdf

14 http://www.webarchive.org.uk/wayback/archive/20140614144831/http://www.jisc.ac.uk/publications/programmerelated/2009/respondingtolearners.aspx

Here are some dos and don'ts to consider when planning your approach:

Do use technology ...	Don't use technology ...	
when it suits the topic	if an online learning package is a substitute for topics where in-depth or face-to-face training would be a better option	*For example, it's better to teach complex skills in the psychomotor domain using face-to-face instruction and coaching, where you can give immediate feedback and physically intervene if necessary.*
when it supports your aims and learning objectives	for the sake of it or to make things easier for you	*For example, do you really need an interactive whiteboard with Internet links to show learners how something works? Why not show them a video or demonstrate it yourself?*
when you can truthfully say that its inclusion will benefit learners	to promote learning as a time or money-saving opportunity for the learner when the quality of your training or learning is likely to suffer	*For example, at-a-distance technologies with no real-time interaction or access to a trainer can be frustrating for learners if they have to wait for feedback on their progress.*
when you know your learners will find it useful or fun	when learners lack the necessary skills to use it without arranging for them to be trained in the required skills first (or if you need to update your own skills beforehand)	*For example, busy learners may welcome the chance to fit online sessions around work and family.*

'We invested in an e-learning package for learners to access at their places of work. The package itself was ideal and covered what our learners need to know. We hadn't factored in our more "difficult" employers – the ones that didn't allow them time to learn. These learners ended up doing the modules at home in their own time, which was demotivating for many of them.'
Training manager

Learning management systems (LMS)

An LMS is also known as a virtual learning environment (VLE) and is a computer-based environment that supports the delivery and assessment of web-based or in-house learning and enables you to interact remotely with your learners. These environments contain different features that allow you to support learners at a distance as well as enabling them to access support and learning resources.

The LMS allows trainers and learners to:

- upload and share learning resources
- work together on activities
- deliver or participate in face-to-face training sessions, either in groups or individually
- assess and track progress
- give and receive feedback on coursework or achievements.

The principal functions of a good LMS are to:

- enable learners to manage their own learning by engaging with their programme at times and in locations that suit them, rather than being constrained by inconvenient attendance requirements

- provide learners with controlled access to resources, which can be imported or produced in house by you and uploaded

- track learner activity and achievement, which allows trainers to set up a learning programme with accompanying resources and activities to direct, guide and monitor learner progress

- support online learning, including access to learning resources, assessment activities and detailed guidance. The learning resources may be developed in house by you, self-developed, or professionally authored and purchased materials that can be imported and made available for learners to use

- allow you to communicate directly with learners to give support and feedback. The LMS also allows learners to communicate with one another and give feedback and peer support. This can be in real time (synchronous) or not (asynchronous).

- provide links to your in-house administrative systems as necessary.

Key point

Using the LMS to build a sense of group identity can be useful when you are dealing with learners who work on their own or who do not have access to their peers.

Smartboards

Also known as interactive boards, smartboards are electronic boards used in the classroom and the workshop that can be linked to the Internet and/or mobile device. They allow you and your learners to interact directly with the board by touching the screen and/or keying in from other devices.

You can use them in a variety of ways:

- **During group work, for keeping track of the group's ideas:** you can move and regroup these by touching the screen and using built-in highlighter tools

- **For note taking:** interactive boards allow you to convert what's written on the board into typed text, which you can either email to learners or print out so that learners can take it away with them in the form of a reminder or handout

- **For playing games:** you can link an interactive board to online games and use the board as a large touchscreen

- **For streaming video and film clips:** linking to live streaming programmes or videos on relevant Internet sites such as YouTube

- **For interactive activities:** these require learners to go up to the board and write, click, drag and/or drop their answers in (good for revision and confirming learning)

- **For slide-show presentations:** you can show your slides and animations via the board and make notes at the same time.

Networking

Most learners already have established personal networks, and social media can therefore provide useful tools for learning. You can use social media sites in two main ways:

- To link up with others for networking purposes (in a user group)

- To upload and share content generated by you and your learners.

Use of social media during sessions could be via learners' own devices or those provided by your organisation, such as computers, laptops and mobile devices. If learners use their own, this saves you having to provide them, but you need to be careful that they are not being used inappropriately. You also need to make sure that everyone has an Internet-enabled device.

The following table shows the advantages and disadvantages of social networks for vocational teaching and learning.

'I ask learners to make a note of one thing they've learned during the session. When I have a large group, I ask learners to write their questions on the board. Others then suggest answers when they come to write theirs up.'
Employability trainer

'Our smartboard has replaced paper flipcharts and handouts. Students download from the screen directly to their handheld devices.'
IT Trainer

Advantages	Disadvantages
They are cheap to use.	There may be issues of security and/or access.
You can use them to create your own groups for the sharing of research findings and/or where infrequent contact is required (for example, a long-term project where everyone in the group comments and contributes).	Many social networking sites do not support the needs of those with physical disabilities – hearing or visual impairments.
Learners who have existing social networks are more likely to use them for learning.	Technophobes won't be using social networks, so don't assume that everyone belongs to one. You may find learners using the technology to access their personal networks rather than any group or network you may have set up, so you will need to manage this carefully.
You can use professional networks such as LinkedIn (www.linkedin.com) as a source of CPD and dialogue between trainers by identifying and joining groups with interests and expertise similar to your own. Similarly, blogs and their associated comment threads are also good ways of reading and contributing to professional discussions.	Quality varies – you need to find groups with special interests similar to yours. You can attract unwanted or 'spam' comments on sites where public access has been enabled. (You can, of course, start your own private group aimed at your learners and control those whom you invite.)

Although most social media networks are easy to get started with, mastering each one for training purposes requires more in-depth knowledge of a particular social media tool and often that of other tools, technologies or specialist software.

Activity: Using digital approaches

When considering digitally based approaches, use the checklist below to help you pinpoint areas to follow up.

Question	Yes	No
1 Does the technology support my aims and learning objectives?	☐	☐
2 Is the technology available in my vocational area?	☐	☐
3 Can learners use the technology?	☐	☐
4 Am I confident about my own ability to use the technology?	☐	☐
5 Does the organisation support the technology (for example, is there access to wifi and/or Internet-enabled devices if appropriate)?	☐	☐
6 Can I justify using the technology (for example, I have considered other ways of delivering)?	☐	☐

You are aiming to answer yes in all cases. If you have answered no to question 1, don't use the technology. If you have answered no to questions 3 and/or 4, you and/or your learners will need to learn how to use the technology first. If you answered no to questions 2 or 5, you will be taking a calculated risk if you decide to go ahead and adopt the technology anyway. If you answered no to question 6, consider your reasons for using the technology first, before going ahead.

Links to the teaching qualifications

Level 3 Award in Education and Training
Unit title: *Understanding and using inclusive approaches in education and training*

Learning outcomes	Assessment criteria
1 Understand inclusive teaching and learning approaches in education and training	**1.1** Describe features of inclusive teaching and learning
	1.2 Compare the strengths and limitations of teaching and learning approaches used in own area of specialism in relation to meeting individual learner needs
	1.3 Explain why it is important to provide opportunities for learners to develop their English, mathematics, ICT and wider skills
2 Understand ways to create an inclusive teaching and learning environment	**2.1** Explain why it is important to create an inclusive teaching and learning environment
	2.2 Explain why it is important to select teaching and learning approaches, resources and assessment methods to meet individual learner needs
	2.3 Explain ways to engage and motivate learners
	2.4 Summarise ways to establish ground rules with learners
3 Be able to plan inclusive teaching and learning	**3.1** Devise an inclusive teaching and learning plan
	3.2 Justify own selection of teaching and learning approaches, resources and assessment methods in relation to meeting individual learner needs
4 Be able to deliver inclusive teaching and learning	**4.1** Use teaching and learning approaches, resources and assessment methods to meet individual learner needs
	4.2 Communicate with learners in ways that meet their individual needs
	4.3 Provide constructive feedback to learners to meet their individual needs

Level 3 Award in Education and Training
Unit title: *Facilitate learning and development for individuals* (Learning & Development unit)

Learning outcomes	Assessment criteria
1 Understand principles and practices of one-to-one learning and development	**1.1** Explain purposes of one-to-one learning and development
	1.2 Explain factors to be considered when facilitating learning and development to meet individual needs.
	1.3 Evaluate methods for facilitating learning and development to meet the needs of individuals.
	1.4 Explain how to manage risks and safeguard individuals when facilitating one-to-one learning and development.
	1.5 Explain how to overcome individual barriers to learning
	1.6 Explain how to monitor individual progress
	1.7 Explain how to adapt delivery to meet individual learner needs
2 Be able to facilitate one-to-one learning and development	**2.1** Clarify facilitation methods with individuals to meet their learning and/or development objectives
	2.2 Implement activities to meet learning and/or development objectives
	2.3 Manage risks and safeguard learners participating in one-to-one learning and/or development
3 Be able to assist individual learners in applying new knowledge and skills in practical contexts	**3.1** Develop opportunities for individuals to apply their new knowledge and learning in practical contexts
	3.2 Explain benefits to individuals of applying new skills
4 Be able to assist individual learners in reflecting on their learning and/or development	**4.1** Explain benefits of self evaluation to individuals
	4.2 Review individual responses to one-to-one learning and/or development
	4.3 Assist individual learners to identify their future learning and/or development needs

Level 3 Award in Education and Training
Unit title: *Facilitate learning and development in groups* (Learning & Development unit)

Learning outcomes	Assessment criteria
1 Understand principles and practices of learning and development in groups	**1.1** Explain purposes of group learning and development
	1.2 Explain why delivery of learning and development must reflect group dynamics
	1.3 Evaluate methods for facilitating learning and development to meet the needs of groups
	1.4 Explain how to manage risks and safeguard individuals when facilitating learning and development in groups
	1.5 Explain how to overcome barriers to learning in groups
	1.6 Explain how to monitor individual learner progress within group development activities
	1.7 Explain how to adapt delivery based on feedback from learners in groups
2 Be able to facilitate learning and development in groups	**2.1** Clarify facilitation methods with individuals to meet their learning and/or development objectives
	2.2 Implement activities to meet learning and/or development objectives
	2.3 Manage risks and safeguard learners participating in one-to-one learning and/or development
3 Be able to assist groups to apply new knowledge and skills in practical contexts	**3.1** Develop opportunities for individuals to apply their new knowledge and learning in practical contexts
	3.2 Provide group feedback to improve the application of learning
4 Be able to assist learners to reflect on their learning and development undertaken in groups	**4.1** Support self-evaluation by learners
	4.2 Review individual responses to learning and development in groups
	4.3 Assist learners to identify their future learning and development needs

Level 4 Certificate in Education and Training
Unit title: *Delivering education and training*

Learning outcomes	Assessment criteria
1 Be able to use inclusive teaching and learning approaches in accordance with internal and external requirements	**1.1** Analyse the effectiveness of teaching and learning approaches used in own area of specialism in relation to meeting the individual needs of learners
	1.2 Create an inclusive teaching and learning environment
	1.3 Demonstrate an inclusive approach to teaching and learning in accordance with internal and external requirements
2 Be able to communicate with learners and other learning professionals to promote learning and progression	**2.1** Analyse benefits and limitations of communication methods and media used in own area of specialism
	2.2 Use communication methods to meet individual learner needs and encourage progression
	2.3 Communicate with other learning professionals to meet individual learner needs and encourage progression
3 Be able to use technologies in delivering inclusive teaching and learning	**3.1** Analyse benefits and limitations of technologies used in own area of specialism
	3.2 Use technologies to enhance teaching and meet individual learner needs
4 Be able to implement the minimum core when delivering inclusive teaching and learning	**4.1** Analyse ways in which minimum core elements can be demonstrated when delivering inclusive teaching and learning
	4.2 Apply minimum core elements in delivering inclusive teaching and learning

Level 4 Certificate in Education and Training
Unit title: *Using resources for education and training*

Learning outcomes	Assessment criteria
1 Be able to use resources in the delivery of inclusive teaching and learning	**1.1** Analyse the effectiveness of resources used in own area of specialism in relation to meeting the individual needs of learners
	1.2 Use resources to promote equality, value diversity and meet the individual needs of learners
	1.3 Adapt resources to meet the individual needs of learners
2 Be able to implement the minimum core when using resources in the delivery of inclusive teaching and learning	**2.1** Analyse ways in which minimum core elements can be demonstrated when using resources for inclusive teaching and learning
	2.2 Apply minimum core elements when using resources for inclusive teaching and learning

4 Assessing learning

The way learners improve their performance or learn more is when you, their trainer, let them know how well they are doing and give them specific help to improve. In addition, the only way you will know whether your training is effective and your learners are achieving the outcomes you have set is to check and assess their work or their performance.

Assessing learning involves two main types of assessment: assessment for learning and assessment of learning, also known as formative and summative assessment. The checking of learning and the effectiveness of your training is known as assessment *for* learning (or formative assessment). By contrast, assessment *of* learning (or summative assessment) involves assessing learners against your in-company standards, service standards, qualification criteria or national standards.

This chapter looks at these two types of assessment, and gives advice on:

- how to incorporate formative and summative assessment into your delivery

- assessment activities to use

- how to give feedback to learners when they have difficulties with their learning.

Assessing in the workplace

Planning for assessment with your learner is key, because you both need to agree in advance on what will be assessed, and how. Where and how you assess will depend on your role. If you work with the learner, this will be relatively straightforward. If you are freelance or working for a training provider, assessment means dealing with a caseload of learners and possibly travelling to different organisations. Arrangements will need to made, many of which involve communicating effectively with a range of other people.

Here are some areas to consider:

- Arranging dates and times that suit you, the learner and their workload

- What will happen if you arrive and the learner is not available (and who pays for your time if you are freelance)

- Being prepared to assess something else if you arrive and the learner is working on something different from what's been agreed

- Gaining permission – for yourself and others involved, such as the IQA – to observe or attend an assessment activity

- Arranging for further, relevant learning and/or assessment opportunities with the employer and/or the learner's supervisor

- Keeping the employer and/or the learner's supervisor informed about the learner's progress and achievements

- Updating the learner's ILP/PLP and any other AO assessment documentation needed.

Key term

Internal quality assurer (IQA):
The person from the centre who is responsible for maintaining and improving the quality of assessment

Assessment for learning

Also called formative assessment, assessment for learning[15] is continual throughout the learning process. This is where you assess the progress the learner is making in their learning during your sessions – checking what they've learned and whether they've understood, how they've learned and whether or not the strategies for their learning are working.

Although the main purpose of formative assessment is to check learner progress, when you find out what works, and what doesn't, you can use this information to inform your teaching or training during subsequent sessions. If several people are involved in assessing the progress of the work-based learner, they all need to communicate and agree on the progress being made, and share this with the learner.

These are the formative strategies to use with your learners:[16]

- Sharing the assessment criteria you're going to use and ways of achieving these with them

- Devising effective strategies for successfully achieving the assessment criteria

- Giving regular feedback that enables them to make progress (see below for more on this)

- Where possible, enabling them to work with their peers as resources for learning

- Providing ways of enabling them to take ownership of their own learning.

---

15 This term was first used by the Assessment Reform Group (1999), *Assessment for Learning: Beyond the Black Box*, Cambridge: School of Education, Cambridge University.

16 Adapted from Marzano, R. (2010), *Formative Assessment and Standards-Based Grading*, Marzano Research Laboratories, Bloomington, IN.

Key point

If you are working towards qualifications, don't automatically adopt the AO's documentation and assume that this will take care of teaching or training needs. Learners don't learn by mindreading, and you should always use active teaching and learning strategies.

'We find it useful for our Level 3 and level 4 learners to access the entire qualification specification before planning for summative assessment, as this allows them to see the whole picture before we break it down into more manageable parts.'
Lead IQA

Examples of methods to assess for learning are:

- regular progress reviews
- oral or written questions
- discussions
- questionnaires
- quizzes
- projects and assignments (written and practical).

Checking progress

Formative assessment involves checking learning and progress during teaching sessions. This means focusing on what your learner is currently doing and whether or not they are understanding what you're showing or teaching them. The mistakes learners might make tell you the sort of help you need to give each individual – or the whole group, if many learners are making similar mistakes. Your job is to offer solutions when they are experiencing difficulties.

Try these steps when helping your learner improve:

1 **When does the problem occur?** Is it that they can't get started or do they have difficulty in applying a new concept in practice?

2 **What's the learning problem exactly?** For example, have they understood what is required of them? Is it that they haven't demonstrated a basic skill and this is preventing them from moving on? Or is it something else? For example, when writing a report, perhaps they don't know what to write or they can't express themselves in full sentences.

3 **Ask the learner where they think their difficulty lies.** Use this as your starting point for giving feedback to the learner about what you think the difficulty is.

4 **Help the learner.** Give them help where they need it, preferably during the session or afterwards if appropriate. Later, check back with the learner that the help you've given is working.

See page 112 for more information on giving feedback.

Assessment for learning activities

On the following pages are some examples of assessment for learning activities that you can adapt for use with learners in your vocational area. Number 1 is from motor vehicle studies, numbers 2 and 3 are from the business and administration sector and number 4 is from customer service. These activities are all structured ways to check learners' knowledge and attitudes.

As you read through each one, see whether you can identify the learning objective the trainer wanted to check when designing the assessment activity. (You'll find suggestions for these on page 112.)

Activity 1 Name the tool

Activity 2 Fill in the blanks

Complete the following sentences, using the correct word from the list below:

Negotiate d............................ and the handover of work – don't just dump it on someone else.

Delegate full responsibility for solving a p............................

Be prompt in forwarding the work so that your colleague has as much time as possible to p............................ it.

Indicate clearly and truthfully how urgent or important the work is so that your colleague can p............................ his or her workload.

Make sure all the necessary i............................ is sent and can be easily understood so that people don't have to keep coming back to you for clarification.

Make sure everything is c............................ before you send it. (If you inherit errors from someone else, make sure they're fixed before the work goes further.)

Make sure work is sent to someone who can h............................, so it isn't delayed while it is repeatedly sent around the company (this happens, especially with email enquiries).

Make r............................ promises to others about response times so that the recipient of the work isn't put under unreasonable pressure.

Offer to help with any further information or c............................ your colleague needs.

process   information   realistic   clarification   prioritise   help   problem   correct   deadlines

Summarising key facts

Your managing director is to make a country trip, going and returning by the same route. You have been given some facts and been asked to write a brief note giving information about the road between Valley and Peak. You are allowed only 120 words, so you may have to leave out some of the facts. Figures count as one word (for example, 3,100).

The basic facts are:

- There are gates at either end of the road and traffic is allowed through only at the permitted times.

- The mouth of the George River was first sighted by Captain James Cook in 1770.

- Last year four cars ran over precipices along the road.

- It is four miles from Valley to the service station.

- Peak is a town at an altitude of 3,100 feet.

- The telephones are free.

- Cars buses, trucks and other vehicles are allowed to leave Peak to go to Valley only between 8am and noon.

- From Peak the road is sealed for the first four miles.

- Halfway up the road there is an extensive and impressive view, which may be seen from a lookout.

- Valley is a town of 570 inhabitants at the mouth of the George River.

- In places the gradient reaches 1 in 6.

- It is 16 miles by road from peak to Valley and back.

- The bulk of the local workforce at Peak is employed in the gold mining industry.

- The total population of Peak is 1,100.

- There is no level road between Peak and Valley.

- No one is allowed to start from Valley to go to Peak between 5 p.m. one day and 1 p.m. the next.

- Cars often overheat on the hill. It is a good idea to see that your radiator has plenty of water.

- Most of the adult males in Valley are employed as commercial fishermen.

- There are vast numbers of trees bordering the road.

- There are three telephones equally spaced along the road, from which you can ring if you are in difficulties.

Taking messages

The following table lists the key items of information you must take when passing on a telephone message. Write down why each item is important. The first has been done as an example.

Key item	What you key in	Why is this important?
Date and time	The date and the time you took the message	So that the person receiving it knows how long ago the message was sent
Taken by	Your full name (as the taker of the message)	
For	The name of the person the message is for	
From	The full name of the person you're talking to, plus their telephone number	
Message	A summary of the message; make it as brief as possible and say what you want the recipient to do (for example, 'Call back tomorrow at 10 a.m.')	

Suggested learning objectives
for the above activities

1   Name nine items of equipment used within the motor vehicle sector.

2   Correctly place eight terms in sentences used in the business admin sector.

3   Select, summarise and organise key items of information using a maximum
    of 120 words.

4   Give five reasons for noting down key items of information when taking
    telephone messages.

Don't worry if you didn't get them exactly right. This activity was to give you
some ideas of how you can use formative assessment with your learners.

Giving feedback on progress

When you're assessing learners' progress in the workplace, you need to be able
to give them effective feedback on their performance so that they know where
they are, how well they are doing, and exactly what they need to do to improve.
The challenge is to give feedback that helps them improve performance while
at the same time maintaining their confidence and motivation. Coaching on
the job, for example, can involve giving feedback to learners as they perform a
specific task, as in this exchange during driver instruction.

Trainer and learner approach the vehicle.

Trainer: *Take me through what you would do.*

(Learner is silent.)

Trainer: *OK – what would you do first?*

Learner: *Get in the driver's cab and start the engine?*

Trainer: *There's something even more important.*

Learner: *Oh – safety checks.*

Trainer: *Yes. The first thing you always do is check the vehicle. What would happen if
this were your test?*

Learner: *An automatic fail.*

Trainer: *Yes. Why's that?*

Learner: *If your vehicle's unsafe, you shouldn't be driving it. And unless you check it
you won't know.*

Trainer: *Exactly. Let's start again. Show me the checks you would make …*

In giving feedback, you need to be specific about two things:

- Telling the learner where they don't meet the requirements, and how.
  For example, 'You didn't use paragraphs when you set out your report.
  This makes it difficult to follow.' Or 'You aren't sorting mail into the
  right departments. This is why the post room is getting complaints.'

- Telling the learner what they need to do next. For example, 'Let's have
  a go at dividing the report up into smaller chunks,' or 'Can you tell me
  the main departments and who works in each one?'

As part of giving feedback, you need to gauge the amount of support your
learner needs. If they haven't quite achieved what they need to achieve, try
asking them questions and guiding them, saying, for example, 'Where's a
good place to end your first paragraph? Show me.' If they can't show you,
this tells you that you may have to set simpler learning objectives or go
back over your training again.

> **Remember**
>
> Make sure the learner understands
> what they have to do and is fairly
> confident that they are able to do it.
> There's nothing more demotivating
> for a learner than telling them to
> try doing a task again if they haven't
> understood it or were unable to do
> what you asked them to do in the
> first place.

Activity: Challenges to learning

Think of a learner or group of learners you currently teach and some of the recent difficulties they have encountered during their learning. Make a note of the clues that suggested to you that they were having difficulties. Then answer the following questions to find out what you need to focus on.

Question	Yes	No	Solution
1 Are the learning objectives clearly understandable and achievable by my learners?	☐	☐	
2 Have I identified what the difficulties are, and how and why they are occurring?	☐	☐	
3 Have I given learners enough individual feedback on their performance?	☐	☐	
4 Should I be adapting my teaching or training?	☐	☐	
5 Is the group difficult to manage?	☐	☐	
6 Does the learner have a particular need or problem?	☐	☐	
7 Is it something else?	☐	☐	

If your answer to question 2 is yes, simplify the tasks; if your answer to question 4 is yes, ask yourself whether you are explaining enough, using the right methods or giving enough individual support. If your answer to question 5 is yes, ask for help with managing the group from a more experienced colleague. If the answer to question 6 is yes, find out what it is and address the problem, by referring the learner for specialist help if appropriate.

'I was asked to run coaching sessions to improve operatives' speed on our production line while maintaining accuracy. I had one learner who would cry as soon as she made the smallest mistake. I asked her how we could find a way forward and it turned out she'd been the victim of bullying in her previous job. Once I knew this, we talked through the best way for me to give her feedback and she was able to start making progress.'
Trainer, manufacturing

Assessment of learning

Also called summative assessment, assessment of learning involves assessing evidence of the learner's knowledge and performance against predetermined standards or criteria, such as those you find in qualifications or organisational key performance indicators (KPIs). The process sums up where the learner is at a given point, and can involve methods such as practical testing or written exams.

Examples of practical methods to assess summative performance are:

- observation
- use of others (sometimes called witness testimony)
- looking for some sort of successful product evidence
- oral questioning.

Examples of practical methods to assess for knowledge are:

- written or online tests and examinations
- multiple-choice tests
- professional discussion
- written assignments, projects and case studies.

Learners often have to complete these knowledge tests and assignments within a certain time limit.

The following table tells you more about the main assessment methods, examples of how they are used, and some of the considerations associated with each one.[17]

> ### Key term
>
> **Product evidence:** The outcomes of the job, such as a successful production run, a word-processed document, a haircut, a meal, or a clean, comfortable and well-fed resident in a care home

---

17 For more information on assessment methods used in work-based learning, see Read, H. (2013), *The best assessor's guide*, Read On Publications.

The main assessment methods

Method	What it means	Good for ...	Other considerations
Observation	Watching learners perform in the workplace	Learners demonstrating their practical skills as they do their job. Most performance-based qualifications specify observation as a primary or mandatory method in their assessment strategies	Risk of observer bias if carried out in isolation from other methods
Discussion (viva)	A conversation with the assessor or with a panel of assessors in which learners describe and reflect on their performance and knowledge in relation to the requirements of the assessment criteria or qualification	Testing the validity and reliability of a learner's knowledge. Can often be used to cover a range of work activities and/or units within a qualification	An effective way to test deep rather than superficial learning, particularly with Level 3 learners and above
Evidence from others (witness testimony)	Another person's account of what a learner has done and/or to confirm their existing knowledge	Supporting an observation and to confirm that the learner has been performing consistently over time	The need to be aware of bias if the witness has a vested interest in the learner succeeding or failing
Questioning	Using a range of questioning techniques, either spoken or written	Finding out whether a learner has the necessary knowledge and understanding behind their performance	The need to avoid using written questions if oral questioning is more appropriate to the areas being assessed, otherwise you are testing learners' literacy
Examining work products	The outcomes or products of a learner's work activity	Using in conjunction with observation, questioning or professional discussion; must be the result of real work	The need to be sure that any products are authentic – the work of the learner – and meet the requirements
Learner statements	The learner's account of what they have been doing in relation to the standards to be achieved	Supporting consistent performance over time, or for evidence of reflection on – and improvements in – performance	A valid method if you are assessing the learner's ability to reflect, or for testing their knowledge, but you wouldn't rely on this method alone as it is subjective to the learner
Recognition of prior learning (RPL)	Assessment of a learner's claim to existing levels of knowledge and skill in relation to the standards within a qualification – usually to avoid the learner having to undergo unnecessary further training and development	Matching prior learning to assessment criteria in a qualification, for example, so the learner doesn't have to repeat what they have already learned	Confirming a learner's claim can involve a number of assessment methods so the assessor can judge whether the evidence they produce is valid, authentic, sufficient and current
Simulation	Using a realistic working environment to assess competence	When it is impossible or unsafe for the learner to perform in a real-life work environment	The risk that the simulation is not valid: how 'real' is it? Also, some qualifications do not permit the use of simulations
Using case studies, projects and assignments	Assessing the outcomes of case studies, projects and assignments that a learner has undertaken as part of their vocational learning against specified criteria	Using in conjunction with questioning or discussion where there are 'gaps' in the learner's evidence or their work activities don't meet the requirements of the assessment criteria	Projects and assignments set as part of the learning process only provide valid evidence of competence if they meet the assessment criteria in question
Skills tests	Formal testing of skills under test conditions	When it forms part of the requirements for independent assessment in certain qualifications or professional routes, usually those where learners need to acquire a range of technical skills before they can perform in the work environment; or for safety-related knowledge and skill requirements	Learners may need to practise under test conditions before undergoing the real thing

Holistic assessment

This is a method of assessing several aspects of a qualification, unit, programme or job specification at the same time. As one piece of good-quality evidence – such as a carefully planned observation or a discussion – could cover several areas, it should be a more efficient and quicker system than assessing aspects separately. Holistic assessment enables learners to integrate knowledge and performance, for example, as part of an apprenticeship programme. It should be planned to enable the learner to know what they need to demonstrate and/or produce by a certain date.

Assessment of a learner's skills, knowledge and understanding can be much more efficient and cost-effective if planned correctly, for both the assessor and learner. Demonstration of a skill often implies the knowledge required to perform that skill, but the use of questions will confirm understanding.

Making assessment decisions

Assessing summatively against preset standards means applying rigorous moderation or standardisation procedures to make sure you and other assessors are arriving at robust assessment decisions in the same ways and are treating learners fairly. By using a range of assessment methods and choosing the most appropriate ones for the purpose, you should be in a position to make firm decisions about the learner's competence against any assessment criteria.

Key terms
Moderation: A way of comparing assessment decisions to either confirm or adjust them
Standardisation: A way of ensuring consistency of assessment decisions between assessors

Activity: Making reliable assessment decisions

You need to ask the following questions to reach a reliable assessment decision at the summative stage:

Is the learner's evidence...	
valid?	Does it meet the learning outcomes and assessment criteria in question?
authentic?	Has the learner produced the evidence on their own? If it's from a group activity, what contribution did the learner make?
current?	Is it up to date?
sufficient?	Is there enough evidence to prove that the learner has demonstrated their knowledge and/or competence over time, under different conditions and to the right level?
Is the assessment method I have chosen ...	
valid?	Is it the right method for the area I am assessing?
reliable?	Is the assessment method or tool I am using likely to produce roughly the same outcome with other learners? (For example, is there a moderation or standardisation process in place to ensure this?)
fair?	Are the methods I am using appropriate to all learners, at the required level, taking into account any particular needs?

For the learner to meet the standards in question, you must be able to answer yes confidently in each case. If you answer no to one or more of the above, this tells you that the learner has not yet met the assessment criteria.

Record keeping and quality assurance

When assessing vocational qualifications, you should keep a detailed, ongoing record (paper-based or electronic) of your assessment decisions and how you reached them. This is an important part of awarding organisation (AO) requirements and of quality assurance of assessment.

Internal quality assurance (IQA)[18] is the process of monitoring the learner journey throughout their time at your organisation by checking the quality of the training and assessment activities the learners undertakes. Without IQA there are risks to the accuracy, consistency and fairness of assessment practice, which could lead to incorrect decisions and ultimately disadvantage the learners.

External quality assurance (EQA) takes place on behalf of an AO to ensure that learners registered with them have received a quality service from the training organisation or centre. EQA also seeks to confirm that assessment and internal quality assurance have been conducted in a consistent, safe and fair manner. However, the EQA role is not just about monitoring: it's also about supporting assessors and IQAs and giving advice and guidance to help them get things right. At some point you might have contact with an external quality assurer – perhaps during a visit, via a remote verification, on the telephone or by email.

Since learners successfully completing a qualification will receive a certificate with the AO's name on, as well as your centre name, the EQA must make sure everything is in order, or their reputation, as well as your centre's, could be brought into disrepute.

---

18 For more information on the roles of the IQA and EQA in work-based learning, see Read, H. (2012), *The best quality assurer's guide*, Read On Publications.

Links to the teaching qualifications

Level 3 Award in Education and Training
Unit title: *Understanding assessment in education and training*

Learning outcomes	Assessment criteria
1 Understand types and methods of assessment used in education and training.	**1.1** Explain the purpose and types of assessment used in education and training **1.2** Describe characteristics of different methods of assessment in education and training **1.3** Compare the strengths and limitations of different assessment methods in relation to meeting individual learner needs **1.4** Explain how different assessment methods can be adapted to meet individual learner needs
2 Understand how to involve learners and others in the assessment process	**2.1** Explain why it is important to involve learners and others in the assessment process **2.2** Explain the role and use of peer and self-assessment in the assessment process **2.3** Identify sources of information that should be made available to learners and others involved in the assessment process
3 Understand the role and use of constructive feedback in the assessment process	**3.1** Describe key features of constructive feedback **3.2** Explain how constructive feedback contributes to the assessment process **3.3** Explain ways to give constructive feedback to learners
4 Understand requirements for keeping records of assessment in education and training	**4.1** Explain the need to keep records of assessment of learning **4.2** Summarise the requirements for keeping records of assessment in an organisation

Level 3 Award in Understanding the principles and practices of assessment
Unit title: *Understanding the principles and practices of assessment* (Learning & Development unit)

Learning outcomes	Assessment criteria
1 Understand types and methods of assessment used in education and training.	**1.1** Explain the functions of assessment in learning and development **1.2** Define key concepts and principles of assessment **1.3** Explain the responsibilities of the assessor **1.4** Identify the regulations and requirements relevant to assessment in own area of practice
2 Understand different types of assessment method	**2.1** Compare the strengths and limitations of a range of assessment methods with reference to the needs of individual learners
3 Understand how to plan assessment	**3.1** Summarise key factors to consider when planning assessment **3.2** Evaluate the benefits of using a holistic approach to assessment **3.3** Explain how to plan a holistic approach to assessment **3.4** Summarise the types of risks that may be involved in assessment in own area of responsibility **3.5** Explain how to minimise risks through the planning process
4 Understand how to involve learners and others in assessment	**4.1** Explain the importance of involving the learner and others in the assessment process **4.2** Summarise types of information that should be made available to learners and others involved in the assessment process **4.3** Explain how peer and self-assessment can be used effectively to promote learner involvement and personal responsibility in the assessment of learning **4.4** Explain how assessment arrangements can be adapted to meet the needs of individual learners
5 Understand how to make assessment decisions	**5.1** Explain how to judge whether evidence is: - sufficient - authentic - current **5.2** Explain how to ensure that assessment decisions are: - made against specific criteria - valid -reliable - fair

6 Understand quality assurance of the assessment process	**6.1** Evaluate the importance of quality assurance in the assessment process
	6.2 Summarise quality assurance and standardisation procedures in own area of practice
	6.3 Summarise the procedures to follow when there are disputes concerning assessment in own area of practice
7 Understand how to manage information relating to assessment	**7.1** Explain the importance of following procedures for the management of information relating to assessment
	7.2 Explain how feedback and questioning contribute to the assessment process
8 Understand the legal and good practice requirements in relation to assessment	**8.1** Explain legal issues, policies and procedures relevant to assessment, including those for confidentiality, health, safety and welfare
	8.2 Explain the contribution that technology can make to the assessment process
	8.3 Evaluate requirements for equality and diversity and, where appropriate, bilingualism in relation to assessment
	8.4 Explain the value of reflective practice and continuing professional development in the assessment process

Level 4 Certificate in Education and Training
Unit title: *Assessing learners in education and training*

Learning outcomes	Assessment criteria
1 Be able to use types and methods of assessment to meet the needs of individual learners	**1.1** Explain the purposes of types of assessment used in education and training
	1.2 Analyse the effectiveness of assessment methods in relation to meeting the individual needs of learners
	1.3 Use types and methods of assessment to meet the individual needs of learners
	1.4 Use peer and self-assessment to promote learners' personal responsibility in the assessment for, and of, their learning
	1.5 Use questioning and feedback to contribute to the assessment process
2 Be able to carry out assessments in accordance with internal and external requirements	**2.1** Identify the internal and external assessment requirements and related procedures of learning programmes
	2.2 Use assessment types and methods to enable learners to produce assessment evidence that is valid, reliable, sufficient, authentic and current
	2.3 Conduct assessments in line with internal and external requirements
	2.4 Record the outcomes of assessments to meet internal and external requirements
	2.5 Communicate assessment information to other professionals with an interest in learner achievement
3 Be able to implement the minimum core when assessing learners	**3.1** Analyse ways in which minimum core elements can be demonstrated in planning assessing learning
	3.2 Apply minimum core elements in assessing learners

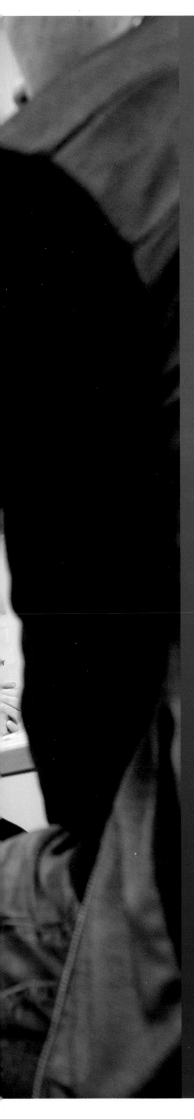

5 Reflecting on performance

As a trainer, you need to reflect on whether or not what you do is working to enhance learning and your learners' experience. Being able to critically reflect on your training means that you see for yourself where you may need to change the way you do things or where you may need help. This ability will be of continuing benefit to your training practice.

The same is true for learners: equipping them with the ability to look critically at their own performance as part of the review process will help them to improve their knowledge and skills and is a vital part of them becoming experts in their chosen fields. It is also a skill which learners can continue to use for their ongoing development long after they have completed their programme.

Reflection is also an important part of your continuing professional development (CPD). To know what your development needs are, you need the ability to stand back from what you do and to reflect critically on what went well, what didn't and what could be improved.

This chapter will:

- help you and your learners with the skills of critical reflection, using examples from other trainers and learners

- tell you how to keep a reflective log, and how you can use it not only to enhance your training but also to identify areas for CPD activities.

The importance of reflection and CPD

In recent years the Government has recognised the importance of CPD, underpinned by skills of critical reflection, in improving teaching. There are professional standards aimed at teachers and trainers that ask you to demonstrate your commitment to the professional values underpinning teaching and training practice. Vocational trainers need to demonstrate how they fulfil their wider professional responsibilities by taking part in professional development to improve their teaching.

The following quote from the introduction to these professional standards underlines the contribution of reflection and CPD to improving performance:

'Teachers and trainers are reflective and enquiring practitioners who think critically about their own educational assumptions, values and practice in the context of a changing contemporary and educational world. They draw on relevant research as part of evidence-based practice. They act with honesty and integrity to maintain high standards of ethics and professional behaviour in support of learners and their expectations.'

Professional Standards for Trainers and Trainers in Education and Training, England, Education and Training Foundation, 2014

The Common Inspection Framework (CIF)

If you are involved in the delivery of government-funded programmes, you will be inspected by Ofsted under the Common Inspection Framework.[19] Four main areas are inspected:

1 Effectiveness of leadership and management

2 Quality of teaching, learning and assessment

3 Personal development, behaviour and welfare (of learners)

4 Outcomes for children and other learners.

You may find it helpful to assess yourself against the criteria below.

Quality of teaching, learning and assessment

Ofsted inspectors will make a judgement on the effectiveness of teaching, learning and assessment by evaluating the extent to which:

- teachers, practitioners and other staff have consistently high expectations of what each child or learner can achieve, including the most able and the most disadvantaged

- teachers, practitioners and other staff have a secure understanding of the age group they are working with and have relevant subject knowledge that is detailed and communicated well to children and learners

- assessment information is gathered from looking at what children and learners already know, understand and can do, and is informed by their parents/previous providers as appropriate

- assessment information is used to plan appropriate teaching and learning strategies, including to identify children and learners who are falling behind in their learning or who need additional support, enabling children and learners to make good progress and achieve well

---

19 Ofsted (2015), *The Common Inspection Framework: education, skills and early years No. 150065.* Available at www.gov.uk/government/organisations/ofsted

- except in the case of the very young, children and learners understand how to improve as a result of useful feedback from staff and, where relevant, parents, carers and employers understand how learners should improve and how they can contribute to this

- engagement with parents, carers and employers helps them to understand how children and learners are doing in relation to the standards expected and what they need to do to improve

- equality of opportunity and recognition of diversity are promoted through teaching and learning

- where relevant, English, mathematics and other skills necessary to function as an economically active member of British society and globally are promoted through teaching and learning.

Key point

Although in-company training and non-government-funded provision are not subject to inspection under the CIF, you might wish to use the criteria for inspection as a useful benchmark for self-assessment of your own practice.

Helping learners to reflect

It isn't easy becoming a reflective learner, but there are benefits of doing so. For workplace learners, the main ones are to:

- encourage routine expertise by helping learners take ownership of their own learning, progress and achievement

- increase motivation by making progress visible to learners.

You may find it helpful to use Donald Schön's[20] ideas on reflection to help your work-based learners improve their performance. Schön believed that most of us possess 'tacit' knowledge, meaning we don't always analyse how or why we perform certain tasks or whether or not these have been carried out well or badly. This is often the case in the workplace, where learners learn tasks by copying their colleagues without necessarily thinking about what they do, or why. Schön identifies two types of reflection: 'in action' and 'on action'.

Reflection in action

This is where you reflect as you carry out a task. This involves analysing what you do as you do it, being critical of yourself, making links to past experiences and learning and thinking ahead to your next activity

If learners are to become competent, it's important to encourage them to reflect in action as they carry out their work activities. One way to do this is to get them to talk themselves through a task in their mind with the aim of improving – say – their speed or accuracy. Or alternatively, get them to talk themselves through a challenging task or problem as they go. You can model the process of talking through a task for them to begin with, using the coaching examples on page 79 as a starting point.

Reflection on action

This involves reflecting on something after it has taken place and might mean realising the significance of a particular event, discussing it with someone else, thinking through what happened, and identifying ways in which you could have done something differently.

You may already ask learners to reflect on action as part of their review process. You will find a written example of a learner reflecting on something they have done on page 127.

---

20 Schön, D. A. (1983), *The Reflective Practitioner*, Basic Books.

What do the following two quotes tell you about each learner?

'When the carer had finished washing and dressing the resident, I asked her: "Why did you knock on the door and close it behind you?" She answered, "Because that's what everyone else does."'

'When the carer had finished washing and dressing the resident, I asked him: "Why did you knock on the door and close it behind you?" He answered, "I don't know. I haven't really thought about it. I think it might be to do with showing respect."'

The first learner has tacit knowledge. She knows what to do, but doesn't know the reasons why. The second learner is starting to think about the reasons why certain procedures might be important. In both cases, however, the learners might not be aware of organisational procedures and might not have been taught about respecting residents' dignity, and haven't reflected on their learning (or a mixture of all three).

Keeping a reflective log

There are many possible ways of reflecting on your practice. It is especially helpful to use reflection to focus on positive and negative incidents that are significant to you and relevant to your training practice. If you are working towards a teaching qualification, you will need to reflect on your progress in a reflective log, diary or journal.

Learners, too, are often required to keep a reflective log or journal as part of their programme of learning or to produce a learner statement as part of the assessment process. As their trainer, you will need to be proactive and teach them how to reflect. A good way to do this is to model a reflective approach yourself.

Triggers for reflection

For you	For learners
A book you have read, or a course or study day you attended	Reflecting on their off-job training day
A training session that went especially well, or badly	An incident at work that they were particularly pleased – or unhappy – about
One of your learners achieving success, or failing	An area of their learning they are enjoying or an occasion at work that made them feel pleased or proud of themselves
Lack of support – or a welcome contribution – from a colleague or colleagues	Praise or criticism for a task that went well – or badly – and how this made them feel
The introduction of a new curriculum, qualification specification, scheme of work or way of working	A new skill they are in the process of learning

Activity: Reflecting on learner needs

The following questions aim to get you thinking about how or whether you meet the needs of your learners.

Question		Yes	No
1	Do you know what motivates each of your learners, and how they prefer to learn?	☐	☐
2	Do the ways in which they like to learn correspond to the delivery strategies you use?	☐	☐
3	Do they see your training as relevant to them?	☐	☐
4	Can you obtain feedback from your learners to help improve your sessions?	☐	☐

What do your answers to the above questions tell you about your training?
Write down your thoughts in your reflective log.

Format and style

Reflective logs can be written down, keyed into a computer, or recorded on an audio device and saved as a sound file. Some people find the latter captures their thoughts better than writing them down.

Both the following examples of reflective logs use a fairly informal, personal style (using 'I', 'we' or 'you'). Some people even use the 'Dear diary' format. You may find it helpful to use a list of questions to focus your thoughts, like the writer of the second extract below. The use of questions stops you losing focus when describing the 'what happened and what do I feel about it?' stages and enables you to move on to reflecting on what you have learnt and what you will do next.

Here are some examples of questions to ask yourself:

- What happened?

- What went well and/or badly?

- What exactly was it that caused this to go so well/badly?

- How do I feel about this?

- What have I learnt?

- What will change?

Remember

Triggers for reflection (sometimes called 'significant events') can be positive things as well as negative ones. They can also be seemingly small incidents as well as large events or situations.

'I think I reflect all the time – but it's all in my head, and then I forget it. Keeping a record is real and helps me to evolve my practice in a more formal way.'
Trainee assessor

Read the following extracts from the reflective logs of a mathematics trainer and an apprentice. The first extract was triggered by a situation with a learner, and the second by the apprentice's observations and frustrations at some of her experiences during the first part of her apprenticeship.

Reflections from a trainer

Reflective log

Observation *(What happened?)*

Today one of my learners, E, sat a Level 2 mathematics test. This was against my advice and that of her other tutor. In our opinion E was not ready for the Level 1 test, let alone the Level 2 test.

As an apprentice, E is funded to complete her vocational qualification at Level 3 and needs to achieve a qualification at Level 2. The problem

is that she is currently working at somewhere between Entry Level 3 and Level 1. She finds mathematics an alien and confusing concept. We could work with E and she will, I'm sure, achieve Level 1. However, it needs to be delivered at her pace and be linked to the job she is currently doing. Her needs do not fit well with a funding deadline.

Reflection *(What went well/badly? How do I feel about it?)*

E sat the Level 2 online test and scored 11 correct answers out of 40, which is around the probability you could expect for guessing at four options per question on a multiple-choice test paper. E admitted that she guessed a lot of the questions and that she hated the whole experience.

I am totally frustrated with the situation, as is the other tutor. There are several issues, which all pose questions:

1. What detrimental effect will this have on E? If we work towards Level 1 we can build her confidence so that she will have a sense of achievement when she passes. E, however, is now demotivated and has lost what little confidence she had. This contradicts all the best practice of treating your learner as an

individual and coaching to success that I know about as a trainer.

2. What initial assessment do we need as a company to avoid enrolling learners on an apprenticeship knowing they will be unable to pass Level 2? A proper initial assessment of each learner is needed before they are accepted on to an apprenticeship. It is not helpful to learners to let them on to a programme they cannot complete.

3. How do I help other staff in the company realise that there is a huge jump from passing L1 mathematics to passing L2? Learners have already had 11 years of education and we need to understand why they have not already achieved.

Review *(What have I learnt?)*

With my business background I appreciate that, as a private training organisation, my company needs to cover costs by maximising funding.

However, as a tutor I find the practice of putting learners through a test they are not ready for unacceptable.

Action *(What will change?)*

The situation has made me realise how important it is for us to ensure that we screen applicants carefully before allowing them on an apprenticeship and that we start to design contextualised activities for practice and embedded projects that will appeal to

employers and can be adapted to their in-house objectives. I will approach the directors with these two concerns. As a company, we need to appeal to employers and provide good-quality tutoring for our learners.

Reflective diary

I have been on my business administration apprenticeship at Anytown District Council for six weeks now. These are my reflections on what I have learnt so far, working in the council tax department dealing with benefits claimants.

What happened?

Today I was on reception, shadowing M, one of the receptionists. She was very busy and was the only receptionist there over the lunch hour. She had to scan in a claimant's proof of address but she wasn't allowed to leave the reception unattended. I offered to help because I had been taught how to scan and upload documents to the system in my first week and I am used to working with technology. But M said I couldn't because reception staff hadn't been trained in how to scan documents by the HR department. I thought this was stupid and I felt annoyed. I was just sitting there and I could have helped.

Another incident was when I had to add notes to claimant's files on the system and sat at D's desk and adjusted her chair. Everyone said I would get into trouble because D does not like anyone sitting in her chair. I don't have a desk! I find this very frustrating as an apprentice and the office junior. I think if you get territorial, everyone else gets nervous and you don't work together as a team.

So what?

These incidents made me realise that departments don't talk to each other and sometimes complain about each other. Also, the chair incident made me realise that people take things personally. I think this is because they are short-staffed and everyone is under pressure.

I saw this when I worked in the post room and staff there refused to sort each department's post because they were so busy. They said we should be sorting our own post. This led to mail being put in the wrong place and not being delivered.

Now what?

I am going to talk to K, my mentor.

1. I will ask if I can have my own desk or if I can share with someone. I definitely don't want to annoy anyone, but I need to have somewhere I can work.

2. I will ask if I can sort the post out in the post room. I do this for our department, which is the biggest, and I would like to learn to sort the others as this will help me to learn about who works for the other departments.

3. I would also like to go out with R, our department's case worker. I am very interested in how council tax assessments are carried out and I think this will give me a break from the office.

Keeping a CPD log

Some activities, such as assessing on behalf of an approved centre, require you to keep a record of your personal development. A CPD log is a record of the activities you've undertaken as part of your professional development. Keeping a log of your CPD activities is not the same as keeping a reflective diary, but your reflective diary will help you identify action points and areas for development that you can use to inform your CPD.

Here's an example of a CPD log kept by a work-based training manager responsible for staff training, who is also undergoing teacher training herself. As you read it, make a mental note of the different types of activity she undertakes.

Date	CPD activity	Learning and information gained	Action taken and application
20 June	Reading: Read, H. (2013), *The best assessor's guide*, Bideford: Read On Publications Topics for teachers of assessors – downloadable resources for those teaching work-based assessors. From: www.readonpublications.co.uk	Background reading and topics for in-house assessor and IQA training	Used content as the basis of my curriculum for assessor and IQA training events
15 August	Reading for teacher-training assignment on reflective practice: Brookfield, S. (1995), *Becoming a Critically Reflective Teacher*, San Francisco: Jossey Bass. Schön, D. A. (1983), *The Reflective Practitioner*, London: Basic Books	Learned how reflective practice underpins professional teaching and the ways in which you can critically appraise your performance	I am using Brookfield's four 'critically reflective lenses' as the basis for critically appraising my own practice. I have started to apply what I am learning within my training.
8 September	Attending a half-day consultation	Future pathways for trainers in the FE sector	Information used to update in-house training events –planning of delivery for 2016
10 September	CPD webinar	Took part in an online discussion and learned about the changes to practice brought about by apprenticeship reforms	Made a note of changes to practice and called a team meeting
15 September	Reading for the teacher training qualification's mandatory units: Gravells, A. and Simpson, S. (2014), *The Certificate in Education and Training*, London: SAGE Publications	Learnt new information about planning, delivering and assessment practices	Tried out some new techniques with my learners in preparation for being observed by my tutor
3 October	Associate trainer review meeting	Feedback from trainers on the in-house events I have run	Made a note of actions to take and future changes to events Will also use comments to inform my own practice

You will have noticed from this log that CPD is about more than attending formal training courses. Examples of other CPD activities include:

- reading – textbooks, professional journals, internal reports, online research
- watching films, DVDs and/or listening to podcasts
- conversations with colleagues, where you learn something and apply it to your own practice. This can include use of social networks.
- attending briefings
- taking on a challenging task or project
- team meetings and standardisation activities (where you learn from other members of the team).

Links to the teaching qualifications

Level 3 Award in Education and Training
Unit title: *Understanding and using inclusive teaching and learning approaches in education and training*

Learning outcomes	Assessment criteria
5 Be able to evaluate the delivery of inclusive teaching and learning	**5.1** Review the effectiveness of own delivery of inclusive teaching and learning
	5.2 Identify areas for improvement in own delivery of inclusive teaching and learning

Level 3 Award in Education and Training
Unit title: *Facilitate learning and development for individuals* (Learning & Development unit)

Learning outcomes	Assessment criteria
4 Be able to assist individual learners in reflecting on their learning and/or development	**4.1** Explain benefits of self-evaluation to individuals
	4.2 Review individual responses to one-to-one learning and development
	4.3 Assist individual learners to identify their future learning and/or development needs

Level 3 Award in Education and Training
Unit title: *Facilitate learning and development in groups* (Learning & Development unit)

Learning outcomes	Assessment criteria
4 Be able to assist individual learners in reflecting on their learning and development undertaken in groups	**4.1** Support self-evaluation by learners
	4.2 Review individual responses to one-to-one learning and development in groups
	4.3 Assist learners to identify their future learning and/or development needs

Level 4 Certificate in Education and Training
Unit title: *Planning to meet the needs of learners in education and training*

Learning outcomes	Assessment criteria
4 Be able to evaluate own practice when planning inclusive teaching and learning	**4.1** Review the effectiveness of own practice when planning to meet the individual needs of learners, taking account of the views of learners and others
	4.2 Identify areas for improvement in own planning to meet the individual needs of learners

Level 4 Certificate in Education and Training
Unit title: *Delivering education and training*

Learning outcomes	Assessment criteria
5 Be able to evaluate own practice in delivering inclusive teaching and learning	**5.1** Review the effectiveness of own practice in meeting the needs of individual learners, taking account of the views of learners and others
	5.2 Identify areas for improvement in own practice in meeting the individual needs of learners

Level 4 Certificate in Education and Training
Unit title: *Assessing learners in education and training*

Learning outcomes	Assessment criteria
4 Be able to evaluate own assessment practice	**4.1** Review the effectiveness of own assessment practice, taking account of the views of learners and others
	4.2 Identify areas for improvement in own assessment practice

Level 4 Certificate in Education and Training
Unit title: *Using resources for education and training*

Learning outcomes	Assessment criteria
3 Be able to evaluate own use of resources in the delivery of inclusive teaching and learning	**3.1** Review the effectiveness of own practice in using resources to meet individual needs of learners, taking account of views of learners and others
	3.2 Identify areas for improvement in own use of resources to meet the individual needs of learners

Index

Order form

To order by post

The best vocational trainer's guide	£35.00	Quantity	Subtotal £
The best assessor's guide	£25.00	Quantity	Subtotal £
The best quality assurer's guide	£30.00	Quantity	Subtotal £
The best initial assessment guide	£30.00	Quantity	Subtotal £
SPECIAL OFFER *Any three assorted guides*	£75.00	Quantity	Subtotal £
Postage & packing 1–2 guides	£4.90*		Subtotal £
Postage & packing 3–4 guides	£8.00*		Subtotal £

* Postage and packing prices correct at time of going to press but may be subject to change.

Total £

Your details

Title	Name
Job title	
Company	
Address	
	Postcode
Telephone	
Email	

Send your order form and cheque made payable to Read On Publications Ltd to:
Read On Publications Ltd, PO Box 162, BIDEFORD, EX39 9DP

To order online, go to www.readonpublications.co.uk
To order by phone, ring the orderline on 0844 888 7138

Lines are open from 9am–9pm Monday to Friday and 9am–5pm, Saturday and Sunday.

Also available from Read On Publications

The best assessor's guide

A guide to good practice for assessors. It contains:

- links to the assessor qualifications and the national occupational standards
- information on choosing the right assessor qualification
- guidance on who does what in assessment
- help with all the assessment methods
- CPD activities for you to develop your practice or that of your team
- advice from experienced assessors on what works and what doesn't.

Using the knowledge and experience of a range of contributors and with many real-life examples, this guide is for anyone working towards an assessor qualification.

The best quality assurer's guide

A guide to good practice for internal and external quality assurers (IQAs and EQAs). It contains:

- links to the qualifications for IQAs and EQAs and the national occupational standards
- information on choosing the right qualification
- guidance on who does what in quality assurance of assessment
- help with sampling and standardisation activities
- CPD activities to use with assessors
- a practical toolkit for IQAs and extra help for Lead IQAs
- advice on how to help centres meet the requirements of the awarding organisation and Ofqual.

Using the knowledge and experience of a range of contributors and with many real-life examples, this guide is for anyone working towards a qualification in quality assurance.

The best initial assessment guide

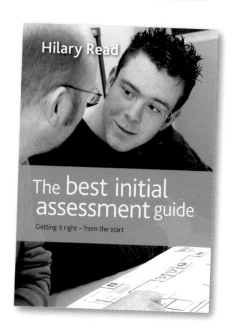

A guide to good practice for those involved in initial assessment, including assessors, vocational trainers and recruiters. It contains:

- advice on designing a robust initial assessment system
- information on choosing and using initial assessment methods
- help on using the results of initial assessment to inform individual learning plans
- guidance on legal compliance
- a process for putting the business case for initial assessment to management.

How to order

By phone: Ring the orderline on 0844 888 7138. Lines are open from 9am–9pm Monday to Friday and 9am–5pm Saturday and Sunday.

By post: Fill in the order form below and send your cheque made payable to Read On Publications to Read On Publications Ltd, PO Box 162, Bideford, Devon EX39 9DP.

Online: Go to www.readonpublications.co.uk

CARDIFF AND VALE COLLEGE